IBERIAN CRIME FICTION

Series Editors
Claire Gorrara (Cardiff University)
Shelley Godsland (University of Birmingham)
Giuliana Pieri (Royal Holloway, London)

Editorial Board
Margaret Atack (University of Leeds)
George Demko (Dartmouth College)
John Foot (University College London)
Stephen Knight (Cardiff University)
Nickianne Moody (Liverpool John Moores University)
Elfriede Müller (Berlin)
Anne White (University of Bradford)

EUROPEAN CRIME FICTIONS

IBERIAN CRIME FICTION

Edited by
Nancy Vosburg

CARDIFF
UNIVERSITY OF WALES PRESS
2011

© The Contributors, 2011

All rights reserved. No part of this book may be reproduced in any material form (including photocopying or storing it in any medium by electronic means and whether or not transiently or incidentally to some other use of this publication) without the written permission of the copyright owner except in accordance with the provisions of the Copyright, Designs and Patents Act 1988. Applications for the copyright owner's written permission to reproduce any part of this publication should be addressed to The University of Wales Press, 10 Columbus Walk, Brigantine Place, Cardiff, CF10 4UP.

www.uwp.co.uk

British Library Cataloguing-in-Publication Data
A catalogue record for this book is available from the British Library.

ISBN 978-0-7083-2332-8
e-ISBN 978-0-7083-2333-5

The right of the Contributors to be identified separately as authors of this work has been asserted by them in accordance with sections 77 and 79 of the Copyright, Designs and Patents Act 1988.

Printed in Great Britain by CPI Antony Rowe, Chippenham, Wiltshire

Contents

1 Introduction to Iberian Crime Fiction — 1
  Nancy Vosburg

2 Crime Fiction since the Spanish Civil War — 6
  Patricia Hart

3 In Search of a New Realism: Manuel Vázquez Montalbán and the Spanish *Novela Negra* — 28
  Mari Paz Balibrea

4 Detecting Difference/Constructing Community in Basque, Catalan and Galician Crime Fiction — 51
  Stewart King

5 Spanish Women's Crime Fiction, 1980s–2000s: Subverting the Conventions of Genre and Gender — 75
  Nancy Vosburg

6 Spanish Crime Fiction: 2001 and Beyond — 93
  David Knutson

7 Five Cases from 130 Years of Portuguese Detective Fiction, 1870s–2000s — 116
  Paul M. Castro

Index — 145

1
Introduction to Iberian Crime Fiction

NANCY VOSBURG

Murder, mayhem and criminal acts of all varieties have been present in the literature of the Iberian Peninsula since its earliest inception (reflected in the twelfth-century epic poem *Cantar de Mío Cid*, for instance), but crime fiction, or *género policíaco*, as we know it today, does not arise on the peninsula until the mid-nineteenth century, a few years after Edgar Allen Poe published 'Murders in the Rue Morgue' (1841) and when a police force identifiable as such was created in Spain. While Spanish Romantic writers such as the Duque de Rivas, with his 'Una antigüalla de Sevilla' (1843, A Seville Antique), and José Zorrilla, with 'Un testigo de bronce' (1845, A Bronze Witness), experimented with crime fiction in verse, Pedro Antonio de Alarcón is generally credited with writing the first crime story in Spain, the 1853 *El clavo* (The Nail).[1] As the story begins, it appears to be a tale of unrequited love between the magistrate/detective, Zarco, and a mysterious woman named Blanca.[2] By the time a murder is discovered, readers anticipate that Zarco's investigation will inevitably lead him back to Blanca, who drove a nail through her previous husband's head. The story is narrated by his friend and companion, Felipe, who has flashes of intuition that foreshadow the outcome. While readers are in the know about 'who done it' because of the way the narrative is set up, Alarcón's story nevertheless presents the logical steps that Zarco takes in his investigation, making it an early precursor to the modern detective novel. The story also includes an interesting twist, unusual for its time, as the magistrate/detective discovers his own role in the chain of events, which forces him to assume some of the responsibility for the crime.

After the 1887 appearance of the British sleuth Sherlock Holmes in *A Study in Scarlet*, imitative works abounded in Spain in penny novels and melodramas.[3] But the genre received a literary boost when the grande dame of Spanish narrative at the turn of the century, Doña Emilia Pardo Bazán, wrote a detective novella, *La gota de sangre* (1911, The Drop of Blood), featuring the amateur sleuth Señor Selva. The protagonist, a wealthy, bored dandy and a suspect in a murder that has occurred outside his home, keeps one step ahead of the local police force when he investigates and solves the crime in order to prove his own innocence. One of the most interesting aspects of this novella is the depiction of the institutional police force, which is shown to be backward, unscientific and thus incapable of carrying out a rigorous murder investigation, a theme which, as Hart documents, recurs even in contemporary detective fiction and is particular to Spain.[4] Additionally, the novella is innovative in its metafictional aspects, as Señor Selva, an avid reader of detective fiction, engages in frequent self-reflection about his actions and methods.[5] And, perhaps most important of all, Pardo Bazán seems much more interested in exploring the motives for the crime than in the means by which the detective discovers the murderer.

Despite the impetus given to the genre by the renowned Pardo Bazán, crime novels were still considered a low-brow form of literature and publicly disdained or dismissed by writers and intellectual readers in Spain in the early decades of the twentieth century. There were a handful of penny novels featuring Spanish sleuths in the 1920s and 1930s, although translations of the British 'cozy' mysteries were more popular. The Catalan novelist Mercè Rodoreda published *Crim*, a parody of the English cozy novel, in 1936, which suggests that she already considered crime fiction a dead genre. Yet, even during the Spanish Civil War (1936–9), three detective novels set in Spain and featuring a Spanish police inspector named Venancio Villabaja were written by E. C. Delmar (pseudonym of Julian Amich Bert): *El misterio del contador* (The Mystery of the Book-keeper), *Piojos grises* (Gray Lice) and *La tórtola de la puñalada* (The Stabbed Turtle Dove).[6] In general, the detective novels of this period, including Delmar's, were imitative of the British cozy mysteries or reworkings of American and English plots.

In Portugal, detective fiction started even more slowly than in Spain, and as Paul Castro points out in his chapter in this volume, was essentially born in parody. Portugal's greatest naturalist/realist writer, Eça de Queiroz, co-wrote with Ramalho Ortigão *O Mistério da Estrada de Sintra* (The Sintra Road Mystery), published in 1870 and considered the first Portuguese detective novel. As Castro notes in his chapter, '*O Mistério* was essentially designed as a hoax. It was, therefore, the first instance of the playfulness that has often characterized the detective fiction genre in Portugal.'

Despite the relatively late appearance of detective fiction in Spain and Portugal, as compared with Great Britain, France and the US, crime fiction enjoys a great popularity in contemporary Iberian literature, with crime novels often topping the best-seller lists in both countries. In this volume, the contributors, all of whom have published articles or books on Iberian crime fiction and have participated in international conferences on the topic, have attempted to identify and explain the high points in the development of the genre, while simultaneously exploring the ways in which the crime novel serves as a vehicle for exploring issues of national concern.

Patricia Hart of Purdue University was the first Hispanist to publish a volume in English on Spanish detective novels, *The Spanish Sleuth*, in 1987. In chapter 2, she considers the somewhat late appearance of crime fiction in Spain. She traces the development of the crime novel as it began to pick up more literary impetus in the 1950s, primarily with the works of Mario Lacruz. Her essay provides an overview of the development of Spanish crime fiction from Lacruz's *El inocente* (1953, The Innocent) to the 1990s.

In chapter 3, Mari Paz Balibrea, of Birkbeck College, University of London, focuses specifically on the *novela negra*, the Spanish manifestation of the hard-boiled detective novel made popular in the US from the 1930s to the 1950s by such authors as Dashiel Hammett and Raymond Chandler. As Balibrea shows, Manuel Vázquez Montalbán, with twenty-three novels in his Pepe Carvalho series, is considered Spain's greatest practitioner of the *novela negra* phenomenon. He was the most significant and most influential writer of the genre from the 1970s until his death in 2003.

In chapter 4, Stewart King of Monash University in Australia explores the ways in which detective fiction in the Spanish autonomous regions with their own distinct languages (Catalonia, Galicia and the Basque Country) is used as a vehicle to promote national identity in these regions and to explore their unique cultural differences compared with the Castilian-dominated centre. King has chosen a representative author from each of the three autonomous regions to demonstrate the concerns of writers from the peripheral regions of Spain.

Nancy Vosburg, of Stetson University in the US, dedicates chapter 5 to the emergence of a large body of women's crime fiction which began in 1980s Spain. As Vosburg reveals in her analyses of women's crime fiction, issues of gender in the masculine-dominated crime genre become of paramount importance as women writers challenge the assumptions of both genre and gender in a rapidly changing society. The chapter also underscores the ways in which women's crime fiction gives us a measure of women's status, and the obstacles they continue to face, in the new egalitarian nation.

David Knutson of Xavier University completes the study of Spanish crime fiction in chapter 6 with his essay on contemporary trends in the genre. Knutson traces the continued presence of some of the writers who pioneered the genre in Spain, and considers new authors who have continued the tradition of the hard-boiled novel, but who bring in more contemporary themes such as anti-globalism, the environment and divergent views of the past, the present and the future. He also demonstrates how contemporary practices of crime writing blend with other cultural trends, such as the continuing interest in historical fiction, particularly the focus on the aftermath of the Spanish Civil War.

The final essay (chapter 7) is dedicated to Portuguese crime fiction, and is written by Paul Castro, currently the Leverhulme Early Career Fellow at the University of Leeds in Great Britain. Castro traces the development of the genre in Portugal from its earliest inception, the 1870 *O Mistério de Estrada de Sintra* by Eça de Queiroz and Ramalho Ortigão, to the present. The chapter concludes with a discussion of contemporary trends in Portuguese crime fiction, which have many points in common with the current trends in Spain while remaining true to Portuguese national character.

Acknowledgements

I would like to thank all of the contributors to the volume as well as Stetson University for providing me with a sabbatical leave to compile this volume.

Notes

[1] Ricardo Landeira, *El género policíaco en la literatura española del siglo XIX* (Alicante: La Universidad de Alicante, 2001), pp. 24–5.
[2] Although it was written in 1853, 'El clavo' was published in a collection of Alarcón's stories entitled *Cuentos amatorios* (Love Stories) in 1881.
[3] Landeira, *El género policíaco en la literatura española del siglo XIX*, p. 18.
[4] Patricia Hart, *The Spanish Sleuth* (London and Toronto: Associated University Presses, 1987).
[5] Landeira, *El género policíaco*, pp. 27–8.
[6] Hart, *The Spanish Sleuth*, p. 25.

Bibliography

Alarcón, Pedro Antonio de, *El clavo* (Alicante: Biblioteca Virtual Miguel de Cervantes, 1999).

Hart, Patricia, *The Spanish Sleuth: The Detective in Spanish Fiction* (London and Toronto: Associated University Presses, 1987).
Landeira, Ricardo, *El género policíaco en la literatura española del siglo XIX* (Alicante: La Universidad de Alicante, 2001).
Pardo Bazán, Emilia, *La gota de sangre*, in Federico Carlos Sainz de Robles (ed.), *Emilia Pardo Bazán: Obras completas* (Madrid: Aguilar, 1957), pp. 994–1014.

2
Crime Fiction since the Spanish Civil War

PATRICIA HART

Introduction

'A murder occurs; many are suspected; all but one suspect, who is the murderer, are eliminated; the murderer is arrested or dies.'[1] Thus W. H. Auden defined the murder-mystery genre in 1948 in his landmark *Harper's* article, 'The guilty vicarage'. 'There is Concealment (the innocent seem guilty and the guilty seem innocent) and Manifestation (the real guilt is brought to consciousness).'[2] Auden's pronouncements are an excellent point of departure for this discussion of Spanish detective fiction from the 1940s to the 1980s, with its late, and sporadic, emergence. Whether murder stories take place in a cosy closed room in a village or on urban mean streets, novels describing them in any form were extremely rare in Spain before the late 1970s.

In his 1948 essay, Auden declared that the most satisfactory traditional mystery story requires a reader with a sort of low-grade, semi-permanent sense of social guilt from which the reading of an ordered, formulaic detective story provides temporary relief. He contrasts it with reading Dostoevsky's *Crime and Punishment*, whose 'effect on the reader is to compel an identification with the murderer which he would prefer not to recognize', or Kafka's *The Trial*, where

> the aim of the hero's investigation is not to prove his innocence (which would be impossible for he knows he is guilty), but to discover what, if anything, he has done to make himself guilty. K, the hero, is in fact, a portrait of the kind of person who reads detective stories for escape.[3]

Auden believed that the driving force behind being able to understand Kafka, Dostoevsky or Agatha Christie was the same: a reader must dwell in a psychological 'guilty vicarage', from which detective novels offered escapism with an imaginary possibility of setting the 'vicarage' right.

The successful resolution of a cozy mystery, writes Auden, is 'the phantasy of being restored to the Garden of Eden'.[4] By contrast, discovering the murderer and putting him or her in the hands of the Spanish criminal justice system – perhaps for garrotting – did not return early Spanish pulp readers to Eden. Before the free elections of 1977, detective stories with happy endings usually had to be set in a real or imagined *somewhere else*.

Most observers of the genre agree that to have a methodical, prescriptive type of novel such as the detective story, with its nostalgia for the bourgeois order, you must have a bourgeoisie and civic order. As Ernest Mandel points out in *Delightful Murder: A Social History of the Crime Story*, 'In feudal and despotic societies, torture was the main means of "proving" crimes and unmasking criminals. Innocents died under torture in horrible pain.'[5] If a society lacks confidence, a detective story that puts the universe right cannot play out satisfactorily. Such a story is unconvincing where the police or the courts may employ torture, rather than science, to arrive at predetermined conclusions. In 1841, when Edgar Allan Poe published 'Murders in the Rue Morgue', the Parisian civil and detective police force, the Sûreté (a model for Scotland Yard and the FBI) had already been in existence for thirty years. In Spain, by contrast, the Spanish Inquisition had been out of commission for only seven years and, indeed, Fernando VII had actually garrotted the last heretic – schoolteacher Cayetano Ripoll – in Valencia on 26 July 1826. When we also recognize the fact that Spanish literacy rates were low throughout the nineteenth and early twentieth century, the question to ask is not why were there no novels of cozy, comforting ratiocination springing forth at that time but, rather, why ever would there be?

As Ernest Mandel has pointed out, the detective story reflects and summarizes the historical progress won by the revolutionary bourgeoisie.[6] Given this, it is unsurprising that in the 1920s and 1930s native Spanish sleuths appeared infrequently, mostly in penny literature. In the confusion of the pre-war years and the destruction of the civil war itself (1936–9), only a few books were published.[7] Forty years of Francoist military dictatorship did little to diminish the population's distrust of the state's ability to detect and punish crime. Therefore, it is not surprising that during the 1940s the few Spaniards who wrote detective novels – usually using English-sounding pseudonyms – set their tales outside Spain, finding that readers still preferred foreign locales for detectives, and the cozy over the hard-boiled, which, at that time, had barely appeared in print in Spain.

There were two exceptions in 1953. One was the publication of what can be seen as a prototypical police procedural, *El charco* (The Puddle), by Tomás Salvador.[8] More significantly, 1953 was the year Mario Lacruz published *El inocente*, which can be read at least in part as a *roman noir* as it contains the portrait of corrupt detection by a policeman.

Mario Lacruz, El inocente *(The Innocent Man), 1953*

El inocente is detective fiction in that it contains a policeman who follows a trail of clues through a dark homicide investigation that leads to the death of the most likely suspect – who, unfortunately, is innocent. We gradually discover that our detective knows the suspect to be innocent all along, but persists in his pursuit of the subject in the hope of personal gain. Indeed, *El inocente* has elements straight out of a Chandlerian world where 'gangsters can rule nations and almost cities . . . [and] where the mayor of your town may have condoned murder as an instrument of money-making . . . because law and order are things we talk about but refrain from practising'.[9] It was simply impossible to make such a statement openly about the police in a police state, therefore, the story is set, not in Spain, but in an unspecified Mediterranean country to avoid problems of censorship.

The plot of *El inocente* is simple. When the book begins, the main character, Virgilio Delise, has been detained by the police and is being taken in a car by a pair of policemen to an unknown destination – presumably to headquarters for interrogation. We are not told why he has been picked up, but we know that he was waiting for the police before they arrived and that he is in a state of extreme agitation. 'Sabía – lo sabía antes de que comenzara todo como en una prevista pesadilla' (He knew it – he knew it even before everything started, as if in a foretold nightmare), we read.[10] But why does Delise know in advance, and more importantly, *what* does he know? Are the police mistaken? We have already been predisposed to think they are by the book's title. Why does he escape and flee, and why does he have, as his brother-in-law describes it, 'vocación de culpable' (a guilty vocation)?[11] This beginning cannot help calling to mind Kafka's *The Trial*. As Auden said in the quotation at the beginning of this chapter, the hero must 'discover what, if anything, he has done to make himself guilty'.

After Delise escapes, he is pursued relentlessly by Inspector Doria, a young, ambitious cop who has been relegated to the backwater town of Escala, presumably because of his grating personality. The word 'escala' when used by a traveller means 'staging post', a place where one goes only to change trains or flights.[12] The town of Escala is just such a staging post in Doria's mind, because his one goal in life is to be promoted back to the asphalt of city streets. When he discovers the body of a man who appears to have died falling down the stairs, the policeman clings desperately to the idea that it may have been murder in the hope that through it he may distinguish himself enough for a transfer. Although the novel narrates his pursuit of Delise, it is an anti-detective story in that the detective's reasoning is used not to solve a crime but, rather, in the deliberately twisted attempt to blame a murder on a man whom he knows to be guiltless. Although up to a point the novel may be said to describe 'mean streets' and show police corruption – as do, of course, the novels of Chandler, Hammett and Chester Himes, for example – it is experimental in form and language.[13] Because of this, Kirsten Thorne quite rightly compares it to the Spanish social novel of the 1950s and 1960s.[14]

Early Catalan contributions to the genre

Mario Lacruz (1929–2000) worked most of his life as an editor in Barcelona, and it is not surprising that we should look there for the next important developments in the genre. Although detective fiction emerged later in Catalonia than in the US or Britain, it came about significantly earlier than in the rest of Spain.[15] The genre of 'lladres i serenos' (thieves and night watchmen) was extremely popular and, moreover, Catalan readers had access to noir writers much sooner than their Spanish compatriots, thanks to a series called *La Cua de Palla*, headed by Manuel de Pedrolo (begun in 1963), which translated the giants of the genre directly into Catalan before they had appeared in Spanish. That series included two novels by Pedrolo himself, but they were not the first detective novels in Catalan.

C. A. Jordana and Antoni Careta i Vidal both published detective works without receiving much attention, but a more successful pioneer and catalyst was Rafael Tasis, who was exiled from Catalonia in 1939 at the end of the Spanish Civil War and returned in 1948, familiar with canonical works in English and in Spanish translations. He wrote three detective works – *La Bíblia valenciana* (1955, The Valencian Bible), *És hora de plegar* (1956, Quitting Time) and *Un crim al Paral·lelo* (A Crime on Paralello Avenue, written in 1944 but first published in 1960) – the last of which is in many ways the most interesting for our purposes. The novel stars journalist Fancesc Caldes of Terassa and police inspector Jaume Vilagut of the Drassanes port district of Barcelona, and tells of a vendor of lottery tickets found strangled in her apartment in 1934. Although the setting and character are supremely Catalan, the genre is a foreign import. Journalist Caldes states his desire to write a thesis on detective fiction, and constantly sprinkles his tale with references to Poe, Sayers, Hammett, Van Dine, Conan Doyle, Leblanc, Simenon, Christie and others.

A much more significant publication took place in 1953.[16] The same year that *El inocente* was published, the multifaceted writer Manuel de Pedrolo ventured into the detective genre with *L'inspector fa tard* (The Inspector is Late), the story of a bank worker who sees his chance to make it rich when the bank is robbed one day, only to find himself in competition with the robbers themselves, as well as the police. In 1958 Pedrolo published *Es vessa una sang fàcil* (Easy Blood is Spilled), a dark depiction of murder. Given that the Catalan language was viewed with suspicion in the rest of Spain and treated with outright repression, it is hardly surprising that neither of those books was translated to Castilian. Following them, and in addition to his other writing, Pedrolo published four other books that Salvador Vázquez de Parga classified as *novela criminal*: *Joc brut* (1965, Playing Dirty), *Mossegar-se la cua* (1968, Biting One's Own Tail), *Pas de ratlla* (1972, No Dividing Line) and *Algú que no hi havia de ser* (1974, Someone Who Shouldn't Have Existed). Nevertheless, Pedrolo declared that he considered only *L'inspector fa tard*, *Joc brut* and *Cua* as detective works.[17]

By far the most famous of these novels is *Joc brut*. The protagonist and first-person narrator, Xavier Rius, is the son of a Republican soldier killed in the war. His problems begin when he falls in love with a beautiful but dangerous Juna, a femme fatale worthy of James M. Cain. She coerces Xavier into committing murder on her behalf, and then abandons him to his fate. Urban squalor and police corruption provide the backdrop.

In *Mossegar-se la cua*, the first-person narrator is a private eye who is asked by a regular and wealthy client, Jordana, to investigate what would appear to be a bizarre practical joke: when he tries to get a routine copy of his birth certificate, Jordana is greeted with the news that he is legally dead. The ensuing investigation, narrated in a laconic style full of sexual tension, stars another innocent drawn to murder by a conniving woman. Again his suffering is presented as disproportionate to his sins.

One of Pedrolo's stated reasons for experimenting with detective fiction was to preserve the Catalan language, which was in very real danger of extermination when he wrote, and also to encourage younger writers to take up genre fiction, as well as 'serious' forms, to that end.[18] Pedrolo felt that he failed in this goal.[19] However, *Joc brut* was translated into Castilian in 1972 by a young admirer of Pedrolo, Jaume Fuster, who published that same year his own first novelistic production in the genre: *De mica en mica, s'omple la pica* (Little By Little, the Basin Fills). The book was dedicated to Philip Marlowe and Sam Spade, but also recognized Rafael Tasis and Manuel de Pedrolo for being brave enough to write detective novels in Catalan.[20] Since Fuster will be addressed in a subsequent chapter, at this point I shall simply note his influence.

Later on, Catalan detective novelists became more common, but several who are important to mention here are Mallorcan Antoni Serra, who has written a series of novels starring Celso Mosquiero, Maria Antònia Oliver (whose Lònia Guiu will be discussed later in this volume), Valencian Ferran Torrent, whose detectives – Toni Butxana, ex-boxer turned private detective, and intrepid journalist Hèctor Barrera – have appeared in five novels to date,[21] and the most well known, Andreu Martín, whose first publications were in Spanish and who will be discussed later in this chapter.

Next, however, I shall consider the writer who for many years was thought of as the pioneer, the first and virtually the only author of Spanish detective fiction, Francisco García Pavón.

García Pavón

Besides being the year in which Mario Lacruz's *El inocente* appeared, 1953 was the year when young author Francisco García Pavón wrote a short story set in the 1920s starring a down-to-earth rural police chief, Manuel González, alias Plinio.[22] Friends liked the story and encouraged the author, who wrote three more short novels, which, however, were not widely distributed until later.[23] When he took up the character again in 1968, it was to write a full-length novel called *El reinado de Witiza* (Witiza's Realm), this time with a contemporary setting. The book won the Premio de la Crítica (Critics' Prize) and was a finalist for the Premio Eugenio Nadal in the same year, and García Pavón followed it in quick succession with *El rapto de las sabinas* (1969, The Rape of the Sabines) and *Las hermanas coloradas* (1970, The Crimson Twins), which were highly successful and were translated into half a dozen other languages. The Plinio novels are the first ones where the rural Spanish *meseta* and its inhabitants are used in simple tales of detection in which mysteries are solved by a hard-working man from La Mancha. The characters speak not in the carefully neutral tones of Mario Lacruz nor in the falsely urbane accents of kiosk detectives translated from English but, rather, in the colorful dialect of Ciudad Real, peppered with earthy curses, jokes and snatches of songs. Patricia O'Connor credits García Pavón with elevating '*la novela policíaca*, a form some consider a sub-species of literature, to a position of respect in Spain'.[24] However, that same year, O'Connor published another article detailing Plinio's machismo ('García Pavón's sexual politics in the Plinio novels'). Although the Plinio novels gained wide popularity, they were relegated to the status of *costumbrista* fiction (or novels of manners), belonging to a second-rate sub-genre.[25] Nevertheless, an early critic, E. Alarcos Llorach, compared García Pavón's work with Balzac, Proust and even Dante in their depiction of the customs of their times.[26]

In any case, and however unjustly, the publication of the Plinio books clearly had a negative effect on how the rest of Pavón's work was received. Only recently have critics begun to re-evaluate his contribution. One of the first of these was Francisco Umbral, who called him 'un proustiano de su pueblo' (a Proustian of his village).[27] José Colmeiro agreed to a large extent, and took up the thread to make an obvious, yet in this case astute and overlooked observation that there was a difference between the author of the stories and the main character. Plinio and his male friends in the rural community, depicted realistically, display a series of attitudes that are sexist, homophobic and xenophobic, and much of the humour of the novels is based precisely on these attitudes. However, Colmeiro rightly observed that the author himself was demonstrably a liberal. He saw these depictions as fecund ground for the author's social criticism, while they seek to entertain, and once again compared their hero to an anachronistic knight errant.

In fact, although a naive reader may laugh at Plinio and his cast of miscreants and neighbours, it is also possible to read the books as social commentaries on a Land Where Time Stood Still, a direct attempt to discuss the clash between old ways and new through the comforting Manichaeism of the cozy detective form, where guilt is discovered and punished. This is possible, in the novels, precisely because Castile is presented as 'backward', and a meta-reading of the works could place them in the company of the authors of the Generation of 98, who described a Spain in crisis after the loss of its last colonies, wondered how to solve the 'problem' that was Spain and, moreover, saw the central plain's poverty and retarded development as typical of Spain's lagging behind the rest of Europe. We remember Antonio Machado's depiction of Castile as a land of 'decrépitas ciudades, caminos sin mesones, / y atónitos palurdos sin danzas ni canciones' (decrepit cities, roads without inns / and astonished bumpkins without dances or songs).[28] A similar note is struck in *El vendimiario de Plinio* (Vintage Plinio) in the following description: 'Tierras de Castilla tan duras, tan áridas. Comidas de Castilla tan pobres, tan devastadoras del cuerpo . . . Toda nuestra historia es un calambre de necesidades' (Castilian lands, so hard, so arid. Castilian foods, so poor, so devastating for the body . . . All our history is a cramp of need).[29] Whether or not this is a revisionist reading of the Plinio novels, it is a fact that no urban detective fiction was really published in Spain until Francoism ended.

In 1974, one of the most unusual and idiosyncratic of the Spanish sleuths makes his appearance in a book called *Tatuaje* (Tattoo). The detective is Pepe Carvalho, Galician by heritage but Barcelonan by birth; private detective by occupation and gourmet by inclination.[30] Vázquez Montalbán is arguably the single most influential author in the development of the hard-boiled private investigator in Spanish fiction, and his work will be discussed at length by Mari Paz Balibrea in chapter 3.

Eduardo Mendoza

In 1975 a novel was published that took the Spanish literary establishment by surprise: an unknown 32-year-old Barcelona lawyer named Eduardo Mendoza produced *La verdad sobre el caso Savolta* (The Truth about the Savolta Case), a novel of sweeping proportions that recreated the revolutionary tension of the Catalan capital in the early twentieth century. The book won the 1975 Premio de la Crítica, and catapulted the author into the ranks of the foremost contemporary Spanish fiction writers. Therefore, many were surprised when he followed it up with *El misterio de la cripta embrujada* (1979, The Mystery of the Enchanted Crypt). This was a short, humorously parodic detective novel whose unnamed sleuth is a paranoid schizophrenic released by the police from a Barcelona psychiatric hospital in order to serve as an informant in a case involving the disappearance of a girl from a posh parochial boarding school and the murder of a tattooed sailor (a pun on Vázquez Montalbán's *Tatuaje*, whose title is, in its turn, an allusion to a popular song of the same name from the 1950s with lyrics by Rafael de León most famously performed by Concha Piquer). The unconventional sleuth, whose aliases are usually based on variations of his psychiatrist's name, prowls Barcelona from its old-moneyed districts to its less salubrious areas, and the plot flows quickly from one demented picaresque adventure to the next.

Because of the popularity of the first novel, Mendoza has to date published two more with the same protagonist, *El laberinto de las aceitunas* (1982, The Olive Labyrinth) and *La aventura del tocador de señoras* (2001, The Adventure of the Ladies' Dressing Table).

Like Don Quixote, the protagonist of Mendoza's three novels is a wise fool, a *loco-cuerdo*, the victim of a literary delusion that causes him to behave in a way that delights readers as it lambasts every possible flaw in Spanish society, taking it from transition to democracy (in the first two books) all the way to the Aznar prime ministership (1996–2004) when the last novel is set. Part of the joke of the last book is that, although the protagonist is no less deluded now than he was earlier, the more conservative Popular Alliance government has forced many mental patients onto the street (much as happened in the United States under the Reagan administration).[31]

Mendoza's parodic detective novels, popular as they are, have not had the effect of diminishing his stature as one of the great contemporary Spanish writers. He is best known for his mammoth 1986 work, *La ciudad de los prodigios* (The City of Miracles), but has written other novels, essays and one play.[32]

The 'mini-boom'

The transition and early years of the socialist government (1982–96) in Spain saw the simultaneous appearance of a number of detective works from such a variety of writers that some have spoken of a 'mini-boom' in detective fiction in the early 1980s. Following in Mendoza's footsteps, a number of 'literary' authors each wrote one detective book. Examples of this would include Lourdes Ortiz's *Picadura mortal* (1979, Mortal Sting) and Fernando Savater's *Caronte aguarda* (1981, Charon is Waiting). Another work that is sometimes also mentioned is Juan Benet's *El aire de un crimen* (1981, The Air of a Crime). It does involve a mysterious murder, as its title would suggest, and it depicts a dark world that includes corruption, crude language and amorality.[33] However, the investigation of the crime is hardly the central thread of the novel, even though, as Colmeiro points out, it is probably the novel by Benet (who is known for an extremely complicated writing style) which is easiest to read, precisely because he does use some of the mechanisms of detective fiction there.[34] To find a genuine, professional, detective writer, we must go back in time and look elsewhere.

Andreu Martín

The first professional sleuth-maker in Spain – that is to say, one who has unapologetically earned his living by writing non-parodic *romans noirs* – is Andreu Martín. Even the wildly successful Vázquez Montalbán is always playing with the genre, always meta-literary, as his habit of continually burning books in his fireplace concretely demonstrates.

Martín, born in 1949 to a working-class family, began producing dark depictions of the mean streets of Barcelona with a stunning ability to make us see and feel the often terrible crimes he creates. Martín's first four books were published by Sedmay, in a series called Círculo de Crimen, which ran from 1979 to 1980 and had the ambitious goal of getting Spanish sleuth-makers into print. The series was plagued by unevenness of the quality of work published (due in part to the fact that some of the novels were commissioned from writers who had succeeded with other types of writing) and it quickly went bankrupt. Martín's contributions to the series are some of the best. The first, *Aprende y calla* (Learn and Shut Up), was published in 1979, and contained a dispassionate look at those who are able to commit violence with absolute sangfroid. Martín's second work, *El Sr. Capone no está en casa* (1979, Mr Capone is not at Home) was a gangster story set in 1930s Chicago, so it is not until his third book, *A la vejez, navajazos* (1980, Slashing Old Age) that we see the introduction of a genuine sleuth, the new recruit Barcelona cop Javier Lallana, who reappears in other books. In 'Shades of green: the police procedural in Spain', Renée Craig-Odders reminds us: 'The relative scarcity of the police novel in Spain also correlates directly to the long standing public perception of the paramilitary police system as the corrupt enforcer of fascist rule under Franco . . .'[35]

Craig-Odders's observations are pertinent to a discussion of Lallana, who represents the first attempt by any writer in the new Spain to get inside the mind of a policeman in a balanced and realistic way.[36] Lallana is human: he forgets key questions during his interrogations but is too proud to make lists, he loses pieces of evidence and daydreams about women when he should be concentrating on police business. Lallana, dark circles under his eyes, reappears briefly in *Prótesis* (1979, Prosthesis), for just long enough to lose a suspect, thus hastening a deadly confrontation between two criminals; and as protagonist of *Si es, no es* (Maybe It Is, Maybe It Isn't) and other novels.

Andreu's police procedurals and crime novels often have a deadly balance of characters that include different types of sleuths: good police officers attempting to solve crimes in a search for justice, bad current and former police officers hoping to silence evidence of their misdeeds (as in *Prótesis*),[37] private eyes working for pay and violent criminals who seek to steal money, avenge being crossed, or simply seek sadistic pleasure (as in *Por amor al arte* (1982, For The Love of Art)). Martín has published several dozen more crime novels for adults since then in both Catalan and Spanish.

No discussion of Martín is complete without reference to his fiction for young readers. Foremost among them is the delightful series of humorous detective novels written in Catalan in collaboration with Jaume Ribera, starring Juan Anguera, alias 'Flanagan', a teenager who solves mysteries for his classmates but often comes up against serious adult crimes, which he solves with the gallantry of Philip Marlowe.[38] The first, *No demanis llobarro fora de temporada* (Never Order Sardines out of Season) won the Premio Nacional de Literatura Infantil y Juvenil (National Prize for Children's Literature) in 1989, and was followed by a number of successful and prize-winning additional titles published almost simultaneously in Catalan and Spanish, and then translated into various other languages. An extremely prolific writer, the professional 'sleuth-maker', Martín promises to add further to this body of work. His novels chronicle both the increase in urban crime and the transition of the police from a repressive Francoist body into an organism of the new democracy (for good and ill).

Juan Madrid

To be complete, a study of the urban detective fiction of changing Spanish life from the 1980s to the present should definitely include the contributions of journalist and novelist Juan Madrid, who has written over forty novels, including the thirteen-volume series, Brigada Central (Central Brigade), which formed the basis for a television series of the same name.[39] He is considered one of the foremost practitioners of the urban European *roman noir*, with work translated into sixteen languages.

Madrid's first books, *Un beso de amigo* (1980, A Kiss By a Friend), *Las apariencias no engañan* (1982, Seeing is Believing), *Nada que hacer* (1984, Nothing to Be Done About It) and *Regalo de la casa* (1986, On the House) introduce us to Toni Romano – ex-boxer, ex-policeman (drummed out of a corrupt force as Francoism stumbled to an end), ex-employee for a private detective agency who in the first book gets by scrounging for odd jobs. Romano's boxing training helps him to withstand beatings, with his head bloodied but unbowed, and the personal code of ethics that drove him from the corrupt police force also makes him immune to frequent offers of employment or reward from the villains he pursues.[40]

Madrid's prolific output, which continues in its almost pure 'noir' form, chronicles urban crime seen through the lens of a slowly evolving police force. Additional novels include *Un trabajo fácil* (1985, An Easy Job), *Cuentas pendientes* (1995, Debts Outstanding), *Malos tiempos* (1995, Bad Times), *Tánger* (1997, Tangier), *Restos de carmín* (1999, Lipstick Stains), *Gente bastante extraña* (2001, Some Pretty Strange People) and *Grupo de noche* (2003, Night Group). Madrid's fiction may be, in many ways, more formulaic than Martín's, but it is as useful or more useful than Martín's for the purpose of illustrating the way in which the noir evolves parallel to greater political openness in the country.

There are a handful of other writers who produced urban mysteries in the late 1970s and early 1980s with settings other than Madrid or Barcelona. One is Julián Ibáñez, a writer from Santander who has set his stories in the north. Another writer of note is Raúl Guerra Garrido. The Basque country is the setting for most of Guerra Garrido's books, including his 1976 Nadal prize-winning novel, *Lectura insólita de 'El capital'* (An Unusual Reading of *Das Kapital*), which tells the story of a Basque industrialist who is kidnapped by an extreme left separatist faction, and has only one book to read to pass the time – Marx's *Das Kapital*. Guerra Garrido's fiction, along with his public criticism of the extremist Partido Nacional Vasco (PNV, Basque National Party) put the author squarely in the sights of ETA (Euskadi Ta Askatasuna, Basque Homeland and Freedom), which resulted in numerous threats and attacks, most notably when the terrorist group ETA blew up his pharmacy in 2000. Guerra Garrido had combined a profession as a pharmacist with his fiction-writing career, and the neighbourhood pharmacy had been in the family for several generations. Nevertheless, he has continued to speak out and write in a variety of fictional forms, including the crime novel. His lifetime of work earned him the Premio Nacional de las Letras Españolas (National Prize for Spanish Letters) in 2006.

Other writers of note include Alfonso Grosso, who began his literary career in 1961 and sometimes wrote about crimes that resulted from the suffocating atmosphere of small-town Andalusian life. With the freedom of speech that came with the transition to democracy, Grosso, who had been a militant member of the Communist Party since 1955, had the liberty to publish books with a Capote-esque attention to cold detail, such as *Los invitados* (The Guests), based on the true-life Galindo crimes. That book, published in 1978, gave a fictionalized solution to a still unsolved real-life mass murder in a *cortijo* (a country home and farm) in the province of Sevilla. The novel was made into a film in 1987 by Víctor Barrera, and starred Lola Flores and Amparo Muñoz. Grosso also wrote a parodic cozy detective novel titled *Otoño indio* (Indian Summer) in 1983.

There are also some comic fictional detectives who appeared in the late 1970s and early 1980s. The most significant is Jorge Martínez Reverte's bumbling journalist, Julio Gálvez, who gets in over his head in Madrid and the Basque country in five novels: *Demasiado para Gálvez* (1979, Too Much for Gálvez; made into a film directed by Antonio Gonzalo in 1980), *Gálvez en Euskadi* (1982, Gálvez in Euskadi), *Gálvez y el cambio del cambio* (1995, Gálvez and the Transition), *Gálvez en la frontera* (2001, Gálvez on the Border) and *Gudari Gálvez* (2005, Gálvez, Basque Soldier). Several other early comic sleuths include Lourdes Ortiz's proto-feminist Barbara Arenas from *Picadura mortal* (1979, Mortal Sting) and Alberto Miralles's Juan Luis, alias 'El Cocido' (the soft-boiled guy) from *Una semana pintada de negro* (1983, A Week Painted Black).

It is not until the late 1990s and early 2000s that the more serious path opened up by Martín and Madrid begins to fill up gradually with novels that can be called 'police procedurals', though the genre clearly reaches its apex in the work of Lorenzo Silva, who crosses the last frontier by writing about a couple of *guardias civiles* (gendarmes), one of them a woman; the pair consists of Sergeant Rubén Bevilaqua ('Vila' for short) and Corporal Virgina Chamorro.[41]

In choosing as protagonists a pair of *guardias civiles*, Silva's series is particularly transgressive. The Guardia Civil, created around the middle of the nineteenth century, was a force historically feared because of unrestrained, brutal control of rural, isolated parts of the country with almost no accountability. The guardsmen were popularly seen as uneducated, rough men unsuited for even the city police forces. The guard's long-standing reputation as reactionary and violently supportive of totalitarian regimes has a long historical basis in fact. In 1873, General Pavia burst into congress with a company of thirty guardsmen, putting an end to the Spanish First Republic; the guard also kept order with an iron hand during the dictatorship of General Miguel Primo de Rivera (1923–9). Most historians believe that members of the Guardia Civil participated in the shooting of Federico García Lorca at the outbreak of the Spanish Civil War (1936–9). The guard was seen as bluntly, brutally supportive under the authoritarian government of General Francisco Franco (1939–75). The corps's violent involvement in politics continued into the fragile new democracy after Franco's death: on 23 February 1981, guard Lieutenant Colonel Antonio Tejero Molina stormed into Congress, pistol in hand and shouting vulgarities, in a failed attempt at a *coup d'état*.

Before Lorenzo Silva, no novelist had attempted to get inside the head of the 'new' guard to look at its difficult transition into a trusted body made up, largely, of dedicated men and women, many of whom had university degrees. Indeed, Bevilaqua has a degree in psychology, which allows him to function as a sort of Sherlock Holmes, deducing guilt and innocence by suspects' demeanour. He is part of the new force, about which it is said that no one wants to see them but when there is a mess, they are the first ones you call.[42] His partner, Chamorro, represents an even further break with tradition – as a woman struggling to serve with honour in a formerly all-male force, many of whose members cast aspersions on her sexual orientation because of her career choice, transforming her name into *machorro*, or 'butch'. In the view of Renée Craig-Odders, 'The series foregrounds both the inherent discord between individual liberty and social responsibility in a democratic society as well as the seemingly incongruous improving perception of the police in Spain.'[43] She sees it as a valuable tool for unpacking long-held prejudices about the force and also public ambiguity towards forces of order under democracy, while at the same time renewing the procedural genre.

Craig-Odders suggests that Silva's novels merge literary traditions with contemporary Spanish reality. For her, Silva's work is clearly superior to everything that has gone before in the new Spanish procedural: 'In the final analysis, despite the world of corruption and greed portrayed, the detective characters created by Silva are not the same two-dimensional alienated individuals as either their hard-boiled foreign or their Spanish predecessors.'[44] Chamorro's role in Silva's fiction opens the door for a fascinating discussion of the development of the Spanish female sleuth. While not the first female detective in Spanish fiction, as we shall see in chapter 5 of this volume, she is the first to be created by a male author.

Conclusion

Throughout this chapter I have given sporadic examples from the 1950s, 1960s and 1970s and a wealth of examples from the 1980s and early 1990s to show that detective fiction could not emerge in a country where the bourgeoisie, industrialization, democracy and reliable police and judicial institutions developed so very late and sporadically, and where repressive regimes or dictatorship were essentially the norm until 1978. I have alluded to the ways in which this contrasted with Britain, the US and France, and shown that the existence of the Francoist police state for almost forty years (1939–75) stunted the development of a cluster of genres (from cozy to the hard-boiled, including police procedurals and 'why-dunnit' narrations of crime by the criminal). Readers tended to reject the notion – indispensable for a 'cozy' novel – of a criminal who is discovered and then turned over to the police as a means of restoring 'order' to the universe. They were slow to accept home-grown procedurals (which had beginnings in the work of Tasis, prototypes in Martín and then flowered fully in the novels of Lorenzo Silva). I have shown that the case of García Pavón's Manchegan rural municipal guardsman, Plinio, was an exception. I have referred to the embryonic beginnings of criminal novels involving ETA, from Raúl Guerra Garrido's *Lectura insólita de 'El capital'* (1976) through Juan Madrid's *Días contados,* to Jorge Martínez's ironic *Gálvez en Euskadi* (1982) and *Gudari Gálvez* (2005). I have also hinted at the forces that retarded development of female detective fiction even further. Thus, in schematic form, the advancing progress of detective genres in Spain from the 1940s through the transition to democracy has been detected.

* * *

Extract from *El vendimario de Plinio* (Vintage Plinio) by Francisco García Pavón

In this passage, we see small-town police chief Manuel González, alias Plinio, and his sidekick, local veterinary surgeon don Lotario, as they ponder a case over beers in the local bar, 'Gol' (so named because it is located directly in front of the soccer field):

If you really looked at it, the whole thing seemed like a theatre of idiots inflated with that strange air called life. There you saw men, their smackers deep in their wine glasses, laughing open-mouthed, munching on crude snacks, puffing smoke from white cigarettes, anxiously scratching their groins as they drank; sticking out their bellies, and stamping their feet with laughter. The television blasted out idiotic ads. A dog licked its parts under the table. A woman, eyes wide open and choking on cooking oil, handed out plates of cheap fried food through a small window. In a corner, some youths wearing very tight trousers spun modern records full blast. Someone left the door open, and the smoke from the tobacco and the cooking food fled the hiss of voices on the grill . . . A blind man with his guide, a sleepy little boy, was selling lottery tickets. Someone bought them short glasses of wine. The blind man tasted his gingerly with the tip of his tongue. Then he savoured it with relish. The boy drank his down in one gulp then slumped down a bit worn out at his master's side. Plinio and don Lotario, sinking ever deeper into their corner, kept on drinking beers and eating fried squid, with cigarettes, looking without speaking.

Francisco García Pavón, *El vendimiario de Plinio* (Madrid: Destino, 1972), pp. 37–8. Translated by Patricia Hart.

Notes

[1] W. H. Auden, 'The guilty vicarage', *Harper's* (May 1948), cited in *The Dyer's Hand* (New York: Random House, 1948), p. 405.
[2] Ibid.
[3] Ibid., p. 412.
[4] Ibid.
[5] Ernest Mandel, *Delightful Murder: A Social History of the Crime Story* (Minneapolis: University of Minnesota Press, 1984), p. 42.
[6] Ibid., pp. 42–3.
[7] E. C. Delmar (pseudonym for Julian Amich Bert) published three detective novels during the war itself, set in Spain: *El misterio del contador de gas*, *Piojos grises* and *La tórtola de la puñalada*. The detective, a police inspector named Venancio Villabaja, is Spanish, but he, his methods and his sidekick, reporter Juan Bandells, all seem transplanted from London (Patricia Hart, *The Spanish Sleuth: The Detective in Spanish Fiction* (Cranbury, NJ, London and Toronto: Associated University Presses, 1987), p. 25.
[8] Salvador (1921–84) was a veteran of the División Azul (a tough unit of Spanish volunteers who served in the German army on the Eastern Front during the Second World War) and later a Barcelona police inspector who wrote over forty books, a number of which were detective or crime novels.
[9] Raymond Chandler, 'The simple art of murder', in *The Simple Art of Murder* (New York: W.W. Norton, 1968), p. 17.

[10] Mario Lacruz, *El inocente* (Barcelona: Bruguera, 1982), p. 10.
[11] Ibid., p. 196
[12] For further detailed and insightful readings of the term 'escala', including its meaning as the musical scales of Delise's avocation as musicologist, the social ladder that Doria attempts to scale and the uphill struggle that is Delise's life as a whole, see José Colmeiro, *La novela policiaca española: Teoría e historia crítica* (Barcelona: Anthropos, 1994), p. 149.
[13] Hart, *Spanish Sleuth*, p. 26; Colmeiro, *Novela policiaca*, p. 141.
[14] Kirsten Thorne, '*El inocente* de Mario Lacruz, novela precursora social-policíaca', *Hispania*, 80 (March 1997), 36.
[15] For more information, see my articles, 'From knight errant to ethical hero to flatfoot: the development of the detective in Catalan fiction', *Catalan Review*, 3, 2 (December 1989), 71–93; 'Time to fold up and die', *Catalan Review*, 7, 7 (1993), 63–70; and chapters 4 and 5 of *The Spanish Sleuth*, on Manuel de Pedrolo, Jaume Fuster etc., pp. 51–83.
[16] Although many point to 1953 as the date of the appearance of Francisco García Pavón, his Plinio makes his first novelistic appearance in his full modern-day persona in *El reinado de Witiza*, published in 1968 – fifteen years later. That is why it is appropriate to discuss García Pavón later.
[17] Personal letter to this author in 1983, included in Hart, *Spanish Sleuth*, p. 61.
[18] 'Em sembla que, quan tenim por de perdre la nostra llengua, més aviat hauríem de voler escriure obres "populars", ja que allò que ens interesa és allunyar el peril d'extinció que correm i no pas deixar únicament obres "significatives" que, un cop eliminates culturalment, seran una pura curisitat' (It seems to me that when we are afraid of losing our language, we have all the more reason to write 'popular' works, since what interests us is to stave off the danger of extinction that we run, rather than leaving only 'significant' works that, once they are eliminated culturally, will be a pure curiosity), Hart, *Spanish Sleuth*, p. 62.
[19] 'Les vaig escriure amb el propòsit de decidir d'altres autors catalans a fer-ne també, objectiu que fracassà' (I wrote them with the purpose of encouraging other Catalan authors to do the same, an objective which failed), Hart, *Spanish Sleuth*, p. 63.
[20] *De mica en mica*, 'Dedicatòries'. 'A Rafael Tasis i Manuel de Pedrolo, que varen tenir la gosadia d'escriure novel·les policíaques en català' (To Rafael Tasis and Manuel de Pedrolo who dared to write detective novels in Catalan).
[21] *Penja els guants Butxana* (1985, Hang Up Your Gloves, Butxana); *Un negre amb un saxo* (1987, A Black Man With a Saxophone); *L'any de l'embotit* (1992, The Year of the Sausage); *Semental, estimat Butxana* (1997, Stud, Dear Butxana. The title plays with the phrase, 'Elementary, my dear Watson' because of the similarity between 'elemental' and 'semental', so a nice loose translation might be 'Studly in Scarlet') and *Cambres d'acer inoxidable* (2001, Chambers of Stainless Steel). Another detective work without Butxana was *No emprenyeu el comissari* (1984, Don't Stir Up the Police

Commisioner). Other novels, though not specifically detective works, include elements of the underworld, murder and detection: *La mirada del tafur* (1997, The Gaze of the Gambler), *La isla del holandés* (2001, The Island of the Dutchman), *Societat limitada* (2002, Incorporated) and *La vida en el abismo* (2004, Life in the Abyss, finalist for the Premio Planeta).

22 'De cómo el Quaque mató al hermano Folión y del curioso ardid que tuvo el guardia Plinio para atraparle' (Wherein Quaque killed Brother Folión, and the curious trick that the rural guard Plinio employed to trap him). The deliberately archaic title echoes the chapter introductions to seventeenth- and eighteenth-century novels).

23 *Los carros vacíos* (1965, The Empty Carts), *El Carnaval* (1968, The Carnival) and *El charco de sangre* (1968, The Pool of Blood). Like the previous story, the novellas take place during the dictatorship of Primo de Rivera.

24 Patricia O'Connor, 'A Spanish sleuth at last: Francisco García Pavón's Plinio', *Hispanófila*, 48 (1973), 47.

25 Literary *costumbrismo* (the fiction of manners) should be understood here to mean a simplified, romanticized, literary or pictorial interpretation of Spanish local everyday life, mannerisms and customs. The term originated in Spain in the nineteenth century.

26 E. Alarcos Llorach, *Anatomía de la lucha por la vida* [Anatomy of the Fight for Life] (Madrid: Castalia, 1982), p. 132.

27 Francisco Umbral, 'Francisco García Pavón (Premio Nadal, 1969)', *La Estafeta Literaria* (1 February 1971), 9.

28 Antonio Machado, 'A orillas del Duero', *Campos de Castilla* (Madrid: Catédra, 2006), p. 104.

29 Francisco García Pavón, *El vendimiario de Plinio* [Vintage Plinio] (Madrid: Hotel Paraíso, 1972), p. 90. This and several other examples are pointed out by Colmeiro, *Novela policiaca*, pp. 151–64.

30 His author had used the same name for a character in a 1972 farcical novel, *Yo maté a Kennedy*, but the development of the well-rounded Carvalho character who makes his living in Barcelona as a private detective first appears in *Tatuaje*.

31 Richard Kim wrote: 'The gutting of public mental health services began with Reagan, first in California where he closed state-funded mental health facilities. As president he cut aid for federally-funded community-run mental health programmes. The result: thousands of more homeless people in California and nationwide and a spike in the prison population', *The Nation*, 1 December 2007, http://www.alternet.org/blogs/healthwellness/69430/, accessed 9 December 2007. Reagan's move was paralleled during the 1980s in the UK by Margaret Thatcher's Care in the Community programme. 'Ceferino,' the protagonist of the novels in question, repeatedly states his opinion of Spain's parallel problem in *La aventura del tocador de señoras*.

32 For more about Mendoza see Hart's chapter, 'Eduardo Mendoza and the hierarchy of humor', in *The Spanish Sleuth*, pp. 101–8; Colmeiro, *Novela*

policiaca, pp. 194–210; and Hart, 'Eduardo Mendoza', in Marta Altisent (ed.), *Dictionary of Literary Biography*, Spain (Farmington Hills, MI: Bruccoli Clark Layman Book, Thomson-Gale, 2005).

[33] Colmeiro, *Novela policiaca*, p. 224.

[34] Ibid., pp. 224–5.

[35] From 'Shades of green: the police procedural in Spain', in Renée W. Craig-Odders, Jacky Collins and Glen S. Close (eds), *Hispanic and Luso-Brazilian Detective Fiction: Essays on the Género Negro Tradition* (Jefferson, North Carolina: McFarland & Company, 2006), pp.103–22. This rephrasing, by Craig-Odders herself, comes from 'Sin, redemption and the new generation of detective fiction in Spain: Lorenzo Silva's Bevilacqua series', *file:/// C:/0D523147/craigg.htm#1*, accessed 6 December 2007. For her, this late appearance 'was reflected in the negative portrayal of the police typical to the detective novels of the post-transition years. In this respect, the police procedural in Spain clearly enters into an ideological and political debate very different from its North American and British counterparts.'

[36] Lallana prefigures, in this sense, Lorenzo Silva's Bevilaqua and Chamorro, to be discussed below.

[37] *Prótesis* tells the story of a bad former cop, El Gallego, who savagely beats a suspect, knocking out his teeth, and Miguel, 'El Dientes', the convict who wears prosthetic teeth which he compulsively polishes as he seeks revenge. The novel was made into a film in 1983 by Vicente Aranda under the title *Fanny Pelopaja*.

[38] *Todos los detectives se llaman Flanagan* (1991); *No te laves las manos, Flanagan* (1993); *Flanagan de luxe* (1994); *Alfagan es Flanagan* (1996); *Flanagan 007* (1997); *Flanagan Blues Banda* (1997), *Sólo Flanagan* (1999), *El diario rojo de Flanagan* (2004). He has also written a wide selection of other books for young readers and children.

[39] Madrid has called the novel series 'una única y gran novela . . . de casi dos mil páginas' (a unique and great novel . . . of close to 2,000 pages). Prólogo, *Flores, el gitano*, 5; quoted in Colmeiro, *Novela policiaca*, p. 255.

[40] For more on his early work, read 'The cruel streets of Madrid (Juan)', in Hart, *Spanish Sleuth*, pp.159–70; and Colmeiro, 'La novela del hampa de Juan Madrid', in Colmeiro, *Novela policiaca*, pp. 246–57.

[41] At the time of writing, the series includes the novels *El lejano país de los estanques* [The Distant Land of Reservoirs] (1998), *El alquimista impaciente* [The Impatient Alchemist] (2000), *La niebla y la doncella* [Fog and the Maiden] (2002) and *La reina sin espejo* [The Queen without a Mirror] (2005); and four short stories published together in 2005 in *Nadie vale más que otro* [No One is Worth More than Anyone Else].

[42] Today, they are primarily responsible for traffic safety and policing of highways, drugs and contraband, customs and airports, safety of prisons and prisoners, weapons licenses and arms control, security of borders and rural areas with fewer than 10,000 inhabitants, bomb squad and explosives,

terrorism, coast guard, police deployments abroad (embassies) and intelligence and counter-intelligence gathering. Summarized from http://en.wikipedia.org/wiki/Guardia_Civil.

[43] Renée W. Craig-Odders, 'Sin, redemption and the new generation of detective fiction in Spain: Lorenzo Silva's Bevilacqua series', file:////C:/0D523147/craigg.htm#1, accessed 6 December 2007.

[44] Ibid.

Bibliography

Alarcón, Pedro Antonio, *El clavo y otros relatos de misterio y crimen* (Barcelona: Fontamara, 1982).

Alarcos Llorach, E., *Anatomía de la lucha por la vida* (Madrid: Castalia, 1982).

Benet, Juan, *El aire de un crimen* (Barcelona: Planeta, 1980).

Auden, W. H., 'The guilty vicarage', *Harper's* (May 1948), cited in *The Dyer's Hand* (New York: Random House, 1948).

Chandler, Raymond, 'The simple art of murder', in *The Simple Art of Murder* (New York: W.W. Norton, 1968); first published as an essay in *The Atlantic Monthly* in 1944, then as a preface to the novel of the same name in 1950.

Colmeiro, José F., *La novela policiaca española: Teoría e historia crítica* (Barcelona: Anthropos, 1994).

Craig-Odders, Renée W., 'Shades of green: the police procedural in Spain', in Renée W. Craig-Odders, Jacky Collins and Glen S. Close (eds), *Hispanic and Luso-Brazilian Detective Fiction: Essays on the Género Negro Tradition* (Jefferson, North Carolina: McFarland & Company, 2006), pp. 103–22.

——, 'Sin, redemption and the new generation of detective fiction in Spain: Lorenzo Silva's Bevilacqua series', file:////C:/0D523147/craigg.htm#1, accessed 6 December 2007.

García Pavón, Francisco, *El reinado de Witiza* [Witiza's Realm] (Barcelona: Destino, 1968).

——, *El rapto de las sabinas* [The Rape of the Sabines] (Barcelona: Destino, 1969).

——, *Las hermanas coloradas* [The Crimson Twins] [(Barcelona: Destino, 1970).

——, *El vendimiario de Plinio* [Vintage Plinio] (Madrid: Destino, 1972).

Grosso, Alfonso, *Los invitados* [The Guests] (Barcelona: Planeta, 1983).

——, *Otoño indio* [Indian Summer] (Barcelona: Planeta, 1983).

Guerra Garrido, Raúl. *Lectura insólita de 'El capital'* [An Unusual Reading of *Das Kapital*] (Barcelona: Destino 1976).

Hart, Patricia, *The Spanish Sleuth: The Detective in Spanish Fiction* (Cranbury, NJ: Associated University Presses, 1987).

—— 'From knight errant to ethical hero to flatfoot: the development of the detective in Catalan fiction', *Catalan Review*, 3, 2 (December 1989), 71–93.

——, 'Time to fold up and die', *Catalan Review*, 7, 7 (1993), 63–70.
——, 'Eduardo Mendoza', in Marta Altisent (ed.), *Dictionary of Literary Biography*, Spain (Farmington Hills, MI: Bruccoli Clark Layman Book, Thomson-Gale, 2005).
Kim, Richard, 'Ronald Reagan's role in the Hillary hostage situation', *The Nation* (1 December 2007), *http://www.alternet.org/blogs/healthwellness/ 69430/*, accessed 9 December 2007.
Lacruz, Mario, *El inocente* [The Innocent Man] (Barcelona: Bruguera, 1982).
Laín Entralgo, Pedro, 'Ensayo sobre la novela policíaca', in his *Ensayos de la crítica y amistad* (Madrid: Espasa, 1948), pp. 75–98.
Machado, Antonio, 'A orillas del Duero', in *Campos de Castilla* (Madrid: Cátedra, 2006), pp. 114–15.
Madrid, Juan, *Un beso de amigo* (Madrid: Sedmay, 1980).
——, *Las apariencias no engañan* [Seeing is Believing] (Madrid: Noguer, 1982).
——, *Nada que hacer* [Nothing to Be Done About It] (Barcelona: Seix Barral, 1984).
——, *Un trabajo fácil* [An Easy Job] (Barcelona: Alfa, 1985).
——, *Regalo de la casa* [On the House] (Madrid: Júcar, 1986).
——, *Hotel Paraíso* (Madrid: Anaya, 1987).
——, *Días contados* [On Borrowed Time] (Madrid: Alfaguara, 1993).
——, *Cuentas pendientes* [Debts Outstanding] (Madrid: Alfaguara, 1995).
——, *Malos tiempos* [Bad Times] (Madrid: Ediciones Lengua de Trapo, 1995).
——, *Tánger* [Tangier] (Madrid: Acento, 1997).
——, *Restos de carmín* [Lipstick Stains] (Madrid: Espasa Calpe, 1999).
——, *Gente bastante extraña* [Some Pretty Strange People] (Madrid: Espasa Calpe, 2001).
——, *Grupo de noche* [Night Group] (Madrid: Espasa Calpe, 2003).
Mandel, Ernest, *Delightful Murder: A Social History of the Crime Story* (Minneapolis: University of Minnesota Press, 1984).
Martín, Andreu, *Aprende y calla*. Madrid: Sedmay, 1979.
——, *A la vejez, navajazos* [Slashing Old Age] (Madrid: Sedmay, 1980).
——, *El Sr. Capone no está en casa* [Mr Capone Is Not at Home] (Madrid: Sedmay, 1979).
——, *Prótesis* [Prosthesis] (Madrid: Sedmay, 1979).
——, *Por amor al arte* [For The Love of Art] (Barcelona: Bruguera, 1982).
——, *Si es, no es* [Maybe It Is, Maybe It Isn't] (Madrid: Planeta, 1983).
——, *No demanis llobarro fora de temporada* [Never Order Sardines out of Season] (Madrid: Alfaguara, 1989).
Martínez Reverte, Jorge, *Demasiado para Gálvez* [Too Much for Galvez] (Madrid, Debate, 1979).
——, *Gálvez en Euskadi* [Galvez in Euskadi] (Barcelona: Anagrama, 1982).
——, *Gálvez y el cambio del cambio* [Galvez and the Transition] (Madrid: Espasa Calpe, 1995).

——, *Gálvez en la frontera* [Galvez on the Border] (Madrid: Alfaguara, 2001).
——, *Gudari Gálvez* [Galvez, Basque Soldier] (Madrid: Espasa Calpe, 2005).
Mendoza, Eduardo, *La verdad sobre el caso Savolta* [The Truth About the Savolta Case] (Barcelona: Seix Barral, 1975).
——, *El misterio de la cripta embrujada* [The Mystery of the Enchanted Crypt] (Barcelona: Seix Barral, 1979).
——, *El laberinto de las aceitunas* [The Olive Labyrinth] (Barcelona: Seix Barral, 1982).
——, *La ciudad de los prodigios* [The City of Miracles] (Barcelona: Seix Barral, 1986).
——, *La aventura del tocador de señoras* [The Adventure of the Ladies' Dressing Table] (Barcelona: Seix Barral, 2001).
Miralles, Alberto, *Una semana pintada de negro* [A Week Painted Black] (Barcelona: Ultramar, 1983).
O'Connor, Patricia, 'A Spanish sleuth at last: Francisco García Pavón's Plinio', *Hispanófila*, 48 (1973), 47–68.
Ortiz, Lourdes, *Picadura mortal* [Mortal Sting] (Madrid: Sedmay, 1979).
Salvador, Tomás, *El Charco* [The Puddle] (Barcelona: Bruguera, 1986).
Savater, Fernando, *Caronte aguarda* [Charon is Waiting] (Madrid: Cátedra, 1981).
Thorne, Kirsten, '*El inocente* de Mario Lacruz, novela precursora social-policíaca', *Hispania*, 80 (March 1997), 31–7.
Umbral, Francisco, 'Francisco García Pavón (Premio Nadal, 1969)', *La Estafeta Literaria* (1 February 1971), 8–9.
Vázquez de Parga, Salvador, *Los mitos de la novela criminal* (Barcelona: Planeta, 1981).
Vázquez Montalban, Manuel *Tatuaje* [Tattoo] (Barcelona: Batlló, 1974).
Wilson, Edmund. 'Who cares who killed Roger Ackroyd? A second report on detective fiction', *The New Yorker* (20 June 1945), in Howard Haycroft (ed.), *The Art of the Mystery Story: A Collection of Critical Essays* (New York: Biblo and Tannen, 1976), p. 390.

3

In Search of a New Realism: Manuel Vázquez Montalbán and the Spanish Novela Negra

MARI PAZ BALIBREA

By the time the dictator Francisco Franco died in 1975, Manuel Vázquez Montalbán was already a key member of the Spanish (and Catalan) anti-Francoist leftist intelligentsia and well on his way to becoming the obligatory cultural reference he would grow to be in the democratic period.[1] He started his career in 1960 as a journalist but it was interrupted two years later when he was imprisoned for fifteen months due to his participation in a political demonstration. During the last fifteen years of Francoism he produced an impressive volume of writings in an array of genres and disciplines. He exercised his pen as a journalist in many different kinds of periodical publications, from *El Español*, his first employer, a newspaper faithful to the regime, to *Triunfo*, the legendary magazine of the plural anti-Francoist left.[2] In addition to this, by 1975 the young Vázquez Montalbán had written substantial essays on culture and politics, several volumes of poetry and a number of avant-garde plays and narratives which he labelled *literatura subnormal* or 'mentally retarded' literature.[3] Not only a prolific and versatile writer, Vázquez Montalbán was also a militant in the Catalan Communist Party (PSUC) and, therefore, someone with profound social and political convictions ready to be conveyed, censorship permitting, through the medium of his writing.

However, for all the many-faceted and surreptitiously political works that Vázquez Montalbán had been producing during the dictatorship, he had stayed away from the realist mode of representation in his fiction and, to a great extent, from the detective novel too. Pepe Carvalho, the detective who was to become one of the most widely read fictional characters in contemporary Spanish literature, appeared for the first time in a *subnormal* novel of 1972, *Yo maté a Kennedy* (I Killed Kennedy), a narrative that bears no resemblance to the noir its author would come to master. Two years later, in 1974, Vázquez Montalbán would write *Tatuaje* (Tattoo), a recognizable whodunnit and the official opening of a Carvalho series that would, after twenty-three volumes, conclude with the death of the author. But the reasons why Vázquez Montalbán decided to move to such a popular genre are more complex than the anecdote he liked to tell about a bet he made with his father-in-law that he could write a detective novel in fifteen days (which he did, *Tatuaje* being its outcome). Let us devote some time to consider the complexity of these reasons. We shall start by establishing the sociological elements that help us understand the boom that the *novela negra* – a kind of detective fiction where the solving of the crime is less important than the representation of the underside of society and the incorporation of a social critique (in other words, the Spanish version of the American hard-boiled genre) – would enjoy in transitional and democratic Spain. What might very well have begun as a one-off attempt at the genre on the part of Manuel Vázquez Montalbán, became an increasingly viable narrative option to pursue in a favourable context. As we do so, it will become clear how the successful encounter between author, industry and public took place.[4]

Some key sociological factors

By 1975 Spain was very close to being a thoroughly modern country, even if differences need to be taken into account between living standards in cities and the countryside. After the initial phase of economic autarchy and the political isolation of 1940s dictatorial Spain, the opening up of the national borders initiated a period of socio-economic modernization, known as the years of *desarrollismo* (very rapid though uneven economic development), that succeeded in creating a substantial middle class, or at least a consumer class, in the most important Spanish cities such as Madrid, Barcelona, Bilbao and Valencia.[5] Indeed, cities and city dwellers were the main beneficiaries in the modernization process. Acting as attraction poles for jobs and industry, cities grew as towns and villages became less and less populated, seeing their younger inhabitants go, never to come back except as holidaymakers. By the 1960s Spanish cities had recovered their status as industrial cities that they had enjoyed prior to the civil war (1936–9). The complexity of modern cities, with their accumulation of wealth, power and population, social tensions and violence, and close sharing of the space, applied once more to Spanish urban areas, turning them into fertile territory in the imagination of the soon to appear Spanish *novela negra*.

Even more relevant for the purposes of the genre, the transition from dictatorship to democracy (1975–82) coincided with a period of global economic crisis. Its impact in Spain would force the shifting of the national economy from the industrial sectors that had developed so rapidly since the 1950s, to the post-industrial ones, with their emphasis on the tertiary economy. The impact of the crisis was mostly felt in cities. As these reinvented themselves as post-industrial urban spaces specializing in the service economy, they still had to deal with the social costs of liquidating their previous configurations: unemployment, violence, fear, alienation from politics and unprecedented consumption, as well as the trafficking and consumption of drugs, particularly amongst the younger generations. The *novela negra*, an urban genre par excellence, would register all of these transformations and social tensions. Throughout the 1980s, the novel-writing careers of authors such as Andreu Martín, Juan Madrid, Manuel Vázquez Montalbán, Carlos Pérez Merinero or Francisco González Ledesma stemmed from the implicit or explicit acknowledgement and critical analysis of these phenomena.

If the conflictive dynamism of Spanish cities made them ripe to become the raw material for noir writers, the publishing industry was equally prepared to absorb the mass production of their manuscripts, and the readership to delight in their irreverent look at democratic Spain's new social realities. Indeed, the laying of the foundations of a democratic state had brought about extensive social change. The rapid acquisition of a series of rights and liberties fundamentally incompatible with authoritarianism, that is, freedom of association, freedom of expression, universal suffrage, popular sovereignty and equality before the law, had an immediate impact on civic society. The newly acquired freedoms would find expression in the cultural field: the hedonistic, nihilistic, iconoclastic practices influenced by a camp aesthetic sensibility of the cultural movements known as the *movidas* in Barcelona, Madrid and Galicia, originally underground and marginal, found themselves being embraced by the authorities as the embodiment of the new spirit of the times. These urban tribes marked the appearance in the realm of media and public visibility of new political, sexual and aesthetic identities that would have been unthinkable before 1975. Most characteristic of these increasingly visible groups was their explicit antipathy vis-à-vis an open political positioning. By refusing to become political subjects through the traditional channels offered by political parties and the periodic casting of a vote, these new social actors embodied the crisis of legitimacy suffered by the modern principle of representativeness that is often cited as a symptom of postmodernity. Although it could be said that while these mechanisms of representation and political participation were old and arguably worn out by European and Western standards, they had hardly been tried in the history of modern Spain, where periods of democratic stability had been few and far between. In hindsight, the refusal of these new collectives to play by the rules of the game did not only bring about political apathy and the renunciation of the right to vote but also made room for new, postmodern, non-institutionalized political forms organized around identity claims, leading to the eventual appearance of social movements in the 1980s.

The literary field incorporated all these social changes in its own way, while it was enjoying its own particular editorial boom. New genres emerged and became popular, amongst them the *novela negra*. The open expression of social critiques, the attack on traditional morals and the hedonistic celebration of life constituted new themes for those practitioners in the literary field. *Películas* and *revistas de destape* (soft-porn films and magazines) saturated the public space in the late 1970s, a phenomenon that can be attributable only to the effects of the long period of repression and tight control of morals enforced by three and a half decades of Catholic dictatorship. The market for women's literature flourished in a climate favourable to giving voice to new social actors who had been silenced previously or under-represented. Specifically within the detective genre, such context helps to explain the attention given at the time to a novel such as Lourdes Ortíz's *Picadura mortal* (1979, Mortal Sting), which puts a woman in the position of the private eye, thereby marking a revision of a genre that had been historically masculinist and misogynist.[6]

New identities and new topics and spaces of cultural expression, in order to become widely visible, required a cultural industry to be in place, one capable of absorbing and responding to a high demand for cultural products. We have already mentioned the rapid process of modernization that Spain underwent in the 1960s. Cultural industries – key to the ideological work of the authoritarian state – had been amongst the most successful participants in the making of this bonanza period.[7] In the transitional context, the content that cultural products were able to convey would certainly change quite radically with respect to the years of dictatorship, but the industry as such, particularly the publishing industry, would remain a very prosperous business. Indeed, the years of the transition witnessed an exponential growth in production for the publishing industry. Closer to our topic, Ramón Acín has documented the growth, from 1979, in the number of publishing houses that devoted special collections to the detective novel, and Vallés Calatrava has investigated the increase in the number of magazines and prizes specializing in the genre.[8]

The making of the Carvalho series: detective fiction as political fiction

Vázquez Montalbán's work was characterized from the very beginning by his interest in and appreciation of popular culture and the popular genres. His analysis of popular and mass culture under Franco is represented most famously in his Triunfo series of articles on the topic, later to be brought together in one volume entitled *Crónica sentimental de España* (1971, Sentimental Chronicle of Spain). In the context of studying the presence and influence of the Marxist German philosopher Theodor Adorno in the work of Vázquez Montalbán, Eugenia Afinoguénova links the *Crónica* to Vázquez Montalbán's idea that it had to be through a positive reassessment of mass and popular culture that the Left was to recuperate its contact with the masses and make them think politically again.[9] She suggests that Vázquez Montalbán's embrace of the detective genre, which began only three years later, was connected to the same political understanding.[10] If in his journalistic and non-fictional endeavours the author had analysed how cultural objects worked in a dynamic and complex way at the level of ideology, the detective genre would provide him with the very tool, not to talk about, but to create popular culture himself and, in this way, to try to influence and politicize the public in a new democratic context.

Enormously versatile, the criminal genre stemmed from a modern tradition of popular and mass literature.[11] It could also speak of a high-brow genealogy in Sophocles' *Oedipus Rex*, the short stories of Jorge Luis Borges or the literatures of modern classics such as Dashiel Hammett, Raymond Chandler, Georges Simenon or Patricia Highsmith, none of which was ignored by Vázquez Montalbán. Having read the classics of the hard-boiled genre, Vázquez Montalbán was aware of the political opportunities that the genre had to offer for the narration of a social critique. Moreover, he thought that the genre offered its practitioners a way out of the crisis of social and political realism that had characterized the ideologically charged literary disputes of the last fifteen years of Francoism.

In the 1950s, social realism had dominated the literary scene for those writers who wanted to oppose the dictatorial regime. Based more or less directly on a Marxist (Lukácsian, to be more precise) understanding of literature as an aesthetic revolutionary tool, Spanish social realism tried to portray, interpret and change a reality of hardship, oppression and underdevelopment that was absent from pro-regime cultural accounts of the Spanish contemporary reality. But the 1960s, in the midst of a context of global and local fragmentation affecting the Marxist Left that had the USSR as its model, saw a breakdown in the political front formed by anti-Francoist writers. Juan Goytisolo, Juan Benet and the members of what Josep Maria Castellet named as the *Novísimos* (Newest) generation, to name but a few, distanced themselves from the tenets of social realism (although some, like Goytisolo, had practised it themselves), which they now perceived as simplistic in its representation of reality, naive in its revolutionary pretensions and of poor literary quality. While for some authors, such as Goytisolo, Luis Martín Santos and Juan Marsé, the distancing from social realism implied a search for new and more efficient formal ways of producing a critical account of their contemporary Spain, for others the dismissal of social realism served as final proof of the irrelevance of trying to mix politics with literature at all. The transitional context of the late 1970s tended to reinforce the distance between literary and political endeavours. The mixing of literature and politics came to be understood as inescapably producing a kind of low-quality literature that had made sense and had been tolerated as a cultural weapon in the fight against the dictatorship but that was pointless now that Spain was a democratic, free country. If that was the case, writers could now focus on what was perceived as being the true task of literature: writing as an aesthetic and/or ludic project. This is how the end of realism was proclaimed as one of the defining characteristics of post-Francoist narrative. Even if in passing, it is worth mentioning that the Spanish crisis of realism that I have just outlined can be seen as an example of the discussions on the end of literature and the exhaustion of genres that epitomize global discourses on postmodernity.

To return to Vázquez Montalbán's interpretation of the Spanish *novela negra*, he saw it as a new form of realism, a revival of the realist mode of representation and the task of writing a novel as a political exercise. This newly reconstituted realism would vindicate, in the transitional and democratic context, the possibility, need and relevance of writing a kind of literature that articulated a social critique, often from a leftist point of view. In other words, the *novela negra* would become a strategic cultural space for the critique of the status quo. But how did Vázquez Montalbán think he could, in the eyes of readers, turn such an obsolete practice, in the minds of many, into an endeavour that was once more relevant and desirable? We have already referred to the way in which the modern development of Spanish cities and the existence of a healthy publishing industry as well as a potential mass readership are key sociological factors for understanding the advent of the *novela negra* phenomenon. To these, one needs to add the ways in which Vázquez Montalbán exploited the narratological and structural possibilities of the genre: the private eye's point of view as the main focalizer of the narrations and the hermeneutical, investigatory structure.

A key to the social critique offered by the American hard-boiled genre was precisely the liminality of the private eye. The detective had to be an outsider in the social structure so that he could plausibly move across the range of social classes, from the rich clients to the petty criminals on the outskirts of the city, in pursuit of an understanding of the social, political and moral implications of the truth of a crime. Vázquez Montalbán's protagonist is a faithful example of this narratological and social position. The protagonist of the series, the private eye Pepe Carvalho, is a hybrid in every sense of the word. The child of Galician immigrants who have moved to Catalonia in search of a more prosperous environment, he embodies the *charnego*, a *mestizo* who has lived in Barcelona most of his life, knows Catalan society and its most unconfessable sins and yet has never identified with it. A private detective in the present of the narratives, he has been in the past a representative of two antithetical positions: a member of the Communist Party and subsequently an employee of the CIA. Bearing in mind that this past corresponds historically with the long period of the Cold War, Carvalho the detective can be understood as a kind of synthesis of the two opposing poles, the capitalist and the communist. Having been a participant in the main social emancipation projects of the twentieth century – democracy and communism – Carvalho comes out of both as a perfectly postmodern *desencantado* (disenchanted) person. His position will always be as critical as it will be distant from his objects of scrutiny, who are (mostly) Spaniards enmeshed in a democratic, late-capitalist society and frequently with a Francoist past to hide, either as fascists or as radical leftists (both equally despised in democratic Spain). He has positioned himself beyond any political commitment but will consistently use his vast knowledge of politics, political economy, Spanish and global history and human nature to solve his mysteries. For example, in a crucial moment in the development of the plot in *Los mares del Sur* [Southern Seas], published in 1979 and winner of the prestigious Planeta prize, Carvalho's point of view describes the physiognomy of a suspect character, Lita Vilardell, in terms of the way her physical traits reveal the bloody origins of the family's great fortune, in this way casting a shadow over her status as innocent:

> Thirty-year-old gray-blue eyes were gazing at Carvalho – eyes inherited by every Vilardell since the founding of the dynasty. The first of the line had been a slave trader, at a time when most people no longer trafficked in slaves. He had returned to his home town with enough money to make himself a Count and pass the title on to his children.[12]

Carvalho is an educated man but a renegade critic of culture, as he considers it responsible for (or at least complicit in) the failure of all liberation projects. He is an iconoclast who refuses to appreciate the chance he was given, as the child of poor immigrants, to educate himself. Nothing in the traits that define his character epitomize better his loathing of culture than the burning of books from his impressive collection to start a fire in his home, which happens at least once in each one of these novels.[13]

While this kind of marginal character could never be at the centre of a conventional family, the secondary characters in the series have been labelled by many as constituting a sort of idiosyncratic family.[14] Carvalho does not have a wife, but he does have Charo, a long-term partner who is a prostitute; he does not have a brother, but he has a secretary-subordinate, Biscuter, an ex-thief turned chef whose relationship with Carvalho becomes more and more complex throughout the series in ways that make one remember that of Don Quixote and Sancho; he does not have a father, but has an old Fascist confidant who works as a shoe-shine man. All of them have in common the fact that they are losers, society victims whom Carvalho has reluctantly agreed to shelter and protect. They represent the most consistent evidence throughout the series that, despite his cold posturing, there is a remnant of ethical behaviour in Carvalho.[15]

Hermeneutic narratives and the vindication of historical memory

The political nature of the Spanish *novela negra* was also facilitated by what I have elsewhere called a hermeneutic structure.[16] The importance of the social element in the writing of Spanish detective fiction authors such as Manuel Vázquez Montalbán, Juan Madrid, Andreu Martín, Maria Antònia Oliver, Alfonso Grosso, Francisco González Ledesma and Jorge Martínez Reverte stemmed from the selection of their topics, the marginal position of their protagonists and the investigatory structure that supported their plots, intent on uncovering events from the past (the crime and its reasons) that had been hidden. This is what I call a hermeneutic narrative. Originating in the practices of the American hard-boiled detective novels, this kind of narrative puts the tools of detection created by the modern state at the service of uncovering the criminality of this very state and/or those who most benefited from it: politicians, businessmen and well-respected professionals. The result is a very rich reading experience: first, unlike the reality that surrounds the reader, the narrative creates a world where a response is given to all questions generated by it; secondly, it offers great entertainment for a mass public in a plot packed with action and adventure. The desire to know, and the satisfaction of this desire, can work as ideological tools of social appeasement to the extent that they quench a thirst for politically, socially, economically or psychologically relevant knowledge of the reader's reality that could be worth pursuing through more productive means. But in a context such as that of the Spanish transition to democracy there was a lot of room for using the investigatory, hermeneutical structure for the purpose of offering a social critique.

What, then, was so objectionable about the transitional period that it merited dissection and critique in the *novela negra*? After all, the death of dictator Francisco Franco in November 1975 put an official end to the authoritarian regime over which he had presided since the end of the civil war he had helped to instigate, and a process of transition to a democratic, liberal state started soon after that. It was not long before remarkable progress had taken place, with such milestones as the legalization of political parties (1976), the calling of general elections (1977), the writing of a constitution (1978) and the declaration of the state as a parliamentary, constitutional monarchy (1978). The relative smoothness and rapidity of these processes has made an international model of this Spanish *Transición* which, having departed from the dark tunnel of bloody Francoism, was able to emerge as a standard liberal democracy in less than ten years. Given the results, one could not but agree that the country was ripe for change and the international actors ready to support the liquidation of that authoritarian anomaly in an otherwise democratic western Europe.

However, all these successes came at a price.The transition to a democratic state was also a political process managed behind closed doors by elites from those parties with parliamentary representation.[17] Their leaders focused on negotiating, rather than breaking with, the previous authoritarian state of which some of them had been a part, and on maintaining social consensus in the midst of a global economic crisis that required a profound restructuring of the Spanish economy. Their deliberations and accords materialized in the Pactos de la Moncloa (Moncloa Agreements, 1977) with the trade unions which, in their call for and enforcement of economic austerity and deflation epitomized the political moderation and economic liberalism that was predominantly driving the Spanish transition to democracy.

The belligerent leftist resistance of the dictatorship period, primarily organized by the Communist Party, was the first casualty in this process. A liberal, tolerant attitude and the open expression of a broadly defined desire for freedom were welcomed as social collective expressions, but more militant positions based on a class analysis of the situation were all promptly silenced. These latter included: the impact that the 1973 global crisis was having on the Spanish economy and the Spanish workers in particular; the expression of the need that justice be made for those millions repressed by four decades of dictatorship; or, on the opposite side of the ideological spectrum, militant positions based on the demand for a political U-turn back to authoritarianism. Virulent mass-mobilizations and the social unrest that had characterized the first two years of the transition to democracy were followed by a kind of massive political apathy known as the disenchantment, *el desencanto*.

The paralysis of the *desencanto* entailed, amongst other things, that the possibility of a collective as well as institutional acknowledgement of the atrocities perpetrated by the dictatorial state was not pursued. Silence and wilful forgetting on the part of Spanish society were politically instrumentalized as social acquiescence with the status quo. The success of the political architects of the *Transición* in minimizing dissent is a case study in the social manufacturing of consensus, even when their impressive record was tarnished at home and abroad by the visibility of the violence inflicted on representatives of the Spanish state by radicalized Basques who continued to disagree with the new configuration of the state, the Estado de las Autonomías (State of Autonomous Communities), and demanded independence.

While social unrest and dissent were thus effectively minimized, even more so as the years went by and especially after the Partido Socialista Obrero Español (PSOE, Spanish Workers Socialist Party) came to power in 1982, symbolic forms of dissent and resistance continued to surface. In the cultural field, the *novela negra* is a good example of this. What is most sociologically relevant about the *novela negra* in the transitional and democratic period is that it took itself as a socially critical space, tuned perfectly to a readership which, in addition to being entertained, was looking for critical tools to navigate a society that was encouraging its citizens to embrace the modernity for which they had longed while suppressing the stimulation of any critical reflection on it and how it had come about.

As far as Vázquez Montalbán was concerned, the elements of historical memory, popular culture and politics were deeply interconnected in his Carvalho works. This author would use the widespread reach of the genre and its investigatory structure to perform successive exercises in the negation of the politics of oblivion. In other words, his detective-fiction novels of the first years of the transition can be understood as using point of view, investigation and detection as tools to identify key elements in the recent history of Spain. The institutional manufacturing of collective amnesia in what has come to be known as the Pacto del Olvido (Pact of Forgetting) and the conversion of Francoists into perfect democrats, and in the transformation of fierce radical leftists into perfectly integrated and moderate citizens would be his preferred targets. Despite the propagation of social consent through official discourses, a leftist thinker such as Vázquez Montalbán dared to dissent: he had his own critically subversive opinion about the way in which political and social issues had been handled during the transition and, in particular, about the way in which the Left had squandered its historical and ideological patrimony. Most perfectly of all, it turned out that the legions of readers who avidly bought his books could not agree more with him. Vázquez Montalbán, through his character Carvalho, became a guru leftist analyst of contemporary politics, his books the perfect critical diagnosis of a society apparently on its way to perfection. Ironically, the more critical he was, the more successful he became and the happier his editors were. In this sense one can talk of detective fiction, and of the work of Vázquez Montalbán in particular, as a cultural phenomenon in the Spain of the period, to the extent that it captured the needs and desires of a large audience. I think José Colmeiro refers to this same phenomenon, but applied more widely to Spanish writers of detective fiction, when he claims that they managed to create a common space, a kind of imagined community, where detective fiction linked different cultural practices and literary traditions for a wide audience.[18]

Having explored the sociocultural and political context that brought about the appearance of the *novela negra* during the Spanish transition to democracy, particularly through a focus on Manuel Vázquez

Montalbán, one of its most important practitioners, who was credited with having imported the hard-boiled genre to Spanish soil, I would like now to spend some time analysing one of the most well-known novels in the Carvalho series, *Los mares del Sur* [Southern Seas].

Case study: Los Mares del Sur *(1979, Southern Seas)*

As already mentioned, *Los mares del Sur* was awarded the Planeta prize, the most popular and most lucrative literary prize in Spain, in 1979. It was the fourth novel to appear in the Carvalho series. While it is true that since the late 1960s Vázquez Montalbán had been a respected up-and-coming intellectual, well known to readers of leftist journals, newspapers and magazines and also the enlightened elite who could appreciate his innovative, avant-garde, *subnormal* writings of the late Francoist period, this novel gave the author a national readership that he had not previously enjoyed. The right cultural climate of a society ripe for reading urban narratives of the detective kind and Vázquez Montalbán's mastery in adapting the genre to Spain's contemporary circumstances in a completely convincing way, together with the widest possible distribution of the novel guaranteed to the winners of the prize, catapulted Vázquez Montalbán to the centre of the Spanish cultural scene, a position that he was never to abandon. From the point of view of his aspirations as an intellectual, *Los mares del Sur* meant that his highly political narratives had found a home in a popular genre that would attract over one million followers for him.

Los mares was, indeed, a perfect example of Vázquez Montalbán's capacity to create a highly entertaining narrative while offering, as we will see, a sharp critique of his historical contemporary moment, the key formula of the series' success. *Los mares* finds Carvalho being hired by the widower of a well-known and wealthy member of Barcelona's industrial and cultural elite, whose stabbed body has recently been discovered, dumped on the outskirts of the city, a year after his disappearance. A piece of paper has been found in his pocket with the following sentence written on it in Italian with a felt-tip pen: 'Più nessuno mi porterà nel sud' (no more will anyone carry me south). As the private eye uncovers the truth, the personality of Stuart Pedrell, the deceased, emerges as that of a tormented character unable to come to terms with his own contradictions: on the one hand, an active member of the Catalan aristocracy with huge economic and increasing political power who devotes his time to running his many businesses; on the other hand, an educated person with strong left-wing leanings and, therefore, someone prepared to launch the harshest of attacks on the social position he himself occupies as a class oppressor. Carvalho will reveal in the end that Pedrell decides finally to overcome his contradictions by leaving all his class privilege behind and going to live incognito with a younger, politically committed working-class lover in a working-class neighbourhood of Barcelona, San Magín. When his lover becomes pregnant, her brother, who is presented as a petty criminal as much as a victim of society, because of an absurd family code of honour, kills Pedrell and disposes of the body. Carvalho will present the facts to his widow and to nobody else, except the reader, and this is the attitude we expect from this character. It is important to understand that Vázquez Montalbán's *novela negra* is never about bringing a criminal before the law of the state, as the ideological issue in these novels is not the restoration of good order represented by such a state but, rather, using crime as a means to dissect its worst contradictions and corruption or, more widely, those of all forms of power.

Carvalho's investigation of Pedrell's life and the contradictions of the different social milieux he had inhabited allow Vázquez Montalbán to present a complex social study of the holders of Catalan economic and political power as well as, on the opposite side of the social spectrum, a representation of the political commitment, the political disenchantment with the course of the *Transición* and the economic hardships caused by increasing unemployment and suffered by those in marginal, working-class neighbourhoods of Barcelona. What the narrative uncovers as Pedrell's deepest secrets are revealed are the contradictions of a whole section of the Catalan and, by extension, Spanish Left, made up in important parts of young members of the enlightened bourgeoisie. Having been radicalized during the last years of Francoism, they had forgotten their political agenda once democracy seemed certain. They had come back to what the author used to call 'the family home' to continue to perpetuate their social roles as members of the dominant classes.

The central metaphor of the novel is that of the south. Its double meaning makes possible the disentangling of the mystery about Pedrell's disappearance and subsequent murder, while it widens the text's representation of the leftist elite that Pedrell epitomizes. On the one hand, the south is a utopian space for the West, an orientalist paradise outside the traps of modern society (an excess of rationalization, subordination of life to economic interests and social conventions, repression of desires). The novel explores its implications in the poetry of T. S. Eliot and Salvatore Quasimodo and through the figure of Gauguin. Being so uncomfortable with himself, Pedrell has read about and spoken frequently of escaping to such an idyllic south. On the other hand, the south is the most impoverished and exploited part of the world, the least favoured by global capitalism. This place is represented in the novel by San Magín, the working-class neighbourhood where Pedrell spends the last months of his life. The wealth of meanings attached to the south, combining literary with geopolitical and socio-economic knowledge of the world, is characteristic of the Carvalho series, and becomes clear in the crucial moment of the novel when the enigma is about to be solved.

Even though the narrative seems for a time to investigate only along the lines of the former kinds of implications of the south to solve the mystery, the key to its resolution will be found the moment an astute Carvalho, who is well acquainted both with the European literary and artistic tradition and with the materialist implications of capitalism and class struggle, is able to connect the two: Pedrell has made San Magín his private paradise in the hope of solving his unbearable class contradictions. In San Magín, Pedrell hoped to be able to leave behind all the preoccupations of a ruthless businessman, all his regrets, and to live as part of the working class, in his own terms, a 'free' person. In the following long quote, Carvalho has gathered around some of his intellectual friends for a big meal in his house: Sergio Beser, a real-life university professor and friend of Vázquez Montalbán who makes a cameo appearance, and Fuster, a business agent. They have just found out that the sentence in Pedrell's pocket comes from a poem by Salvatore Quasimodo. Beser explains:

> The lament of a southerner who realizes that he is powerless to return south. His heart has remained in the green fields and overcast waters of Lombardy.
>
> 'It's almost a social poem. Very little ambiguity. Not very polysemic, as *Tel Quel* would say. This collection was published shortly after the war, at the height of critical neo-realism. Just think: "The south is tired of carting round corpses . . . tired of loneliness, of chains . . . tired of the blasphemies of those whose shouts of death have echoed in its wells, who have drunk the blood from its heart." There is amorous counterpoint to the poem: in revealing his sadness as an uprooted southerner, he is speaking to the woman he loves . . . Is this of any use to you?'
>
> Carvalho re-read Stuart Pedrell's sheet of paper.
>
> 'Just literature, in other words.'
>
> A drop of contemptuous spittle flicked from his lip.
>
> 'Yes, I would say so. Just literature. It's amazing the obsession that people have about the south. Maybe it meant something before the days of

tour operators and charter flights, but now the south no longer exists. The Americans have built a literary mythology out of nothing, and the south owes its very existence to them. The word "south" has a primal meaning for every North American. It's their accursed place, their vanquished territory in a land of conquerors; the only defunct white civilization in the United States – the Deep South. Everything follows from that...'[19]

This moment in the novel is a good synthesis of the most important elements in the narrative strategies of the Carvalho series. It is inserted as a piece of high, almost pedantic literary and historical knowledge and, at the same time, it moves the plot of this crime story forwards. Without this information linking literature and art to history, it would be impossible for Carvalho, in the subsequent chapter of the book, to come to the conclusion that Pedrell's south was the working-class neighborhood of San Magín. In this way the fragment, as the whole book does, provides enjoyment for the reader at two levels: critical knowledge of reality and advancement of the plot.

Some conclusions

Due to its immediate connection to contemporary society, the Carvalho series has frequently been labelled a chronicle of the Spanish transition. In effect, one can follow through these books the changes in the social, spatial and political make-up of the city, Barcelona, where the majority of the novels are set, as well as the social and cultural changes (from literature, music, cuisine and politics to sex) affecting Spanish society as a whole. Furthermore, the series spanned more than three decades, with twenty-three titles published, the last one posthumously in 2004, and offers a panoramic view of Spanish society during the greater part of the country's existence as a modern democracy.

Since this set of novels sustained for so long a close focus on the representation of contemporary Spanish society according to the author's own perception of it, it is no surprise that the tone of the series and the topics it addressed change with time. During the late 1970s and the 1980s the narratives were mostly occupied with offering a critique of a country coming out of authoritarianism and, in the process, forgetting its painful past while enjoying a newly found romance with (post) modernity and wealthy Europe. The last example of this kind of narrative is *Quinteto de Buenos Aires* (1997, The Buenos Aires Quintet) to the extent that the plot is concerned with the uncovering of a hidden, bloody and shameful historical, collective past. But, significantly, the action no longer takes place in Barcelona or in Spain; it has moved to Argentina and that country's own difficult process of dealing with a dictatorial past and a transition to democracy.

As we approached and entered the 1990s, the Carvalho series focused more and more on the impact of globalization in Spain, and more specifically on Barcelona. Titles such as *El delantero centro fue asesinado al atardecer* (1989, translated as *Offside*), *El laberinto griego* (1991, The Greek Labyrinth), *Sabotaje Olímpico* (1993, An Olympic Death) or *El hombre de mi vida* (2000, The Man of My Life) critically analysed the impact of post-industrialism in the Catalan capital and its newly found source of identity, wealth and global promotion in the Olympic games and in tourism. It becomes noticeable, too, that the author was more and more interested not only in the social, economic and political implications of globalization in Spain, but also in political developments taking place throughout the world, as the location of *Quinteto* illustrates. Moreover, the abundance of the author's cultural production, without diminishing, stopped being centred on the Carvalho series as the end of the millennium approached, signalling that the series was coming to an end. In fact, the death of the author in 2003 coincided with the publication of what had already been decided would be Carvalho's last adventure, *Milenio Carvalho* (2004, Carvalho Millennium). This novel, in which Carvalho and Biscuter go on a trip around the world and have a chance to witness at first hand the defining conflicts of a new century in turmoil, is closer to the adventure than to the detective genre.

The exhaustion of the Carvalho series can be explained by its close dependence on the logic of its main character, whose point of view dominated the social representation offered by the series. The veracity of the Carvalho novels, their author thought, demanded that the protagonist age as years went by. As Carvalho got older, his pessimism and social voyeurism increased, which has prompted many critics to connect the series to issues of *desencanto* and postmodernism. Nevertheless, it should be remembered that it is not only through the privileging of a point of view, in this case that of Carvalho, but also through the investigatory structure, that the series conveys its meanings. It should also be mentioned that other characters, particularly Biscuter, originally his sidekick and a secondary figure clearly, gained in significance as Carvalho became more and more incapable of dealing with a world for which he thought there was no hope. The culmination of this process occurs in *Milenio*, where Biscuter reveals himself as a fully articulated character, ready to engage with the world and to move on from his dependence on Carvalho. Conversely, his boss becomes so radically disenchanted after his trip around the world that his tragic end in a prison in Barcelona, separated for good from the outside world, hardly comes as a surprise.[20]

As Carvalho leaves the stage, we readers are confronted with the end of one of the most emblematic and influential cultural phenomena of the Spanish democratic period. New historical and social contexts had produced the need and the space for new narratives. During this time, the detective genre that followed the formula inaugurated by *Tatuaje* in 1974 has diversified and flourished in many directions. The Carvalho series, however, disappears as the key figure of its main character becomes useless as a critical point of view. The own logic in the evolution of his personality makes him more and more disengaged with the world around him. Carvalho's contradictory traits as an 'anarchist individualist, as well as a liberal Marxist' as Bayó Belenguer puts it, had served Vázquez Montalbán well as an incisive point of view from which to observe and dissect contemporary Spain.[21] However, Carvalho grew increasingly tired of dealing with the dark and rotten side of society, and it is this disengagement with detection and its social function, rather than a change in opinion about the world around him, that marks the end of this private eye. His author, Vázquez Montalbán, would never move away from the practice of a socially engaged literature, but sought it in other written forms. At any rate, his literary existence of almost thirty years deserves to be credited for having pioneered for the Spanish scene one of the key cultural forms of a generation.

Andreu Martín, Juan Madrid or Francisco González Ledesma, who all started to write in the genre in the late 1970s and the early 1980s, followed closely Vázquez Montalbán's lead or contributed to its success. They all exploited the detective genre as the perfect medium for uncovering and understanding the relation between violence and crime on the one hand, and the social system as a whole in the context of the transition to democracy in Spain's big cities on the other. This is the case in Martín's *Prótesis* (1980, Prosthesis) or *Si es, no es* (1983, Maybe It Is, Maybe It Isn't), Madrid's *Las apariencias no engañan* (1982, Seeing is Believing) or *Regalo de la casa* (1987, On the House), Martínez Reverte's *El mensajero* (1980, The Messenger) and *Gálvez en Euskadi* (1983, Gálvez in Euskadi) and González Ledesma's *Las calles de nuestros padres* (1984, The Streets of Our Parents) and *Crónica sentimental en rojo* (1984, Sentimental Chronicle in Red).

Vázquez Montalbán's clever use of what I have called the hermeneutic structure intrinsic to detective fiction to show how the past is indispensable in solving mysterious crimes of the present is a formula used repeatedly since the 1980s.[22] Antonio Muñoz Molina's *Beltenebros* (1983, Prince of Shadows) and *El jinete polaco* (The Polish Horseman), Pedro Casals's *¿Por qué mataron a Felipe?* (1985, Why Did They Kill Felipe?) and Fernando Savater's *Caronte aguarda* (1981, Charon is Waiting) (all by authors not exclusively connected to the noir genre) are good examples of it.[23] More recently, this interest in the exploration of history through the medium of detective fiction has made a comeback in the context of what is known as the 'memory boom', a period starting in the late 1990s of intense collective debate over the Spanish twentieth-century violent past. Amongst the many cultural representations and interpretations on this topic, one can cite the work of Dulce Chacón's *Cielos de Barro* (2000, Clay Skies), José Javier Abasolo's *Nadie es inocente* (1998, No One is Innocent) and Andrés Trapiello's *Los amigos del crimen perfecto* (2003, The Perfect Crime Club).[24] It would be too simplistic to credit Vázquez Montalbán with having been the inspiration for each and every one of these authors to write their books. However, the far-reaching and enduring influence of topics and cultural forms which he had started to put into circulation back in the 1970s attests to Vázquez Montalbán's outstanding quality as an indispensable cultural practitioner of his time.

* * *

Excerpt from *Los Mares del Sur* (Southern Seas) by Manuel Vázquez Montalbán

In the following fragment, Pepe Carvalho interrogates one of Stuart Pedrell's business partners, an immensely rich Marquess of Munt. In the course of the conversation, they talk about Pedrell, but also about politics and food:

The Marquess of Munt was relaxing on a sofa, with a perfectly composed air of gravity. Seventy years of snobbish living were condensed in the thin frame of a fair-skinned, smartly dressed old man, with eyes like shining slots in which a pair of malignant pupils danced and darted. The lilac veins in his lightly made-up face had been raised like scratch marks by the wine that was keeping cool in the ice bucket. He held a glass in his right hand, and a copy of Michel Guérard's *Cuisine Minceur* in the left. The book beckoned to Carvalho to sit down on any of the lumps that emerged from the milky landscape . . .

'Drink, Señor Carvalho, before the wine comes to an end, before the world comes to an end. Remember what Stendhal said: you do not know what it means to live unless you have lived before the revolution.'

'Are we living before the revolution?'

'Without a shadow of a doubt. A revolution will come soon. Its shape still has to be decided. But it will come. I know, because I have devoted a lot of time to political science'...

'Have you been as imaginative in your business life?'

'It hasn't been necessary. While my father was alive, it was all plain sailing. He respected my personality. He knew that I was creative and that I needed to change my life and other people's. When he died, I was nearly fifty years old, and came into an absolutely staggering inheritance. I put a lot of it into fixed-interest securities, so that I could live like a prince for the rest of my life. I used some more to compensate my wife for bearing me five children, and I made them my heirs. With the remainder, I set myself up in business, always using fellows like Planas or Stuart Pedrell. Fellows with drive, with a fierce ambition for power, but with the possibility of gaining only economic power.'

'You'd be ready to defend your heritage by every available means. Even war.'

'I don't know. It depends. Not if it was a very dirty war. Although I suppose that any war can be made to look attractive. But no, I don't think that I'd come round to supporting violence'...

'Stuart Pedrell tried to escape from his condition. You take yours on, and try to turn it into an aesthetic. Planas is the only one who works.'

'He's the only one who's alienated, although he doesn't recognize it himself. I've tried to help him. But he has the balance of an unbalanced mind. The day he looks in the mirror and says, "I'm mad", he'll fall apart'...

He poured Carvalho some more wine and filled his own glass to the brim.

'It was a Goytisolo novel, *Distinguishing Marks*, which taught me to drink white wine between meals. White wine was also used to sensational effect in the Resnais film *Providence*. Until then, I'd always stuck to strong-bodied ports and sherries. But this is a real blessing. It's also the alcoholic drink with the fewest calories – if one excludes beer. Which white wine do you drink?'

'*Blanc de blancs*, Marqués de Monistrol.'

'I don't know it. I'm a fanatic for Chablis. This one in particular. And if it can't be Chablis, then let it be an Albariño Fefiñanes. It's an impressive hybrid, with roots in Alsace of Galicia. One of the best things they brought us along the road from Santiago de Compostela.'

'Did you have anything in common with Stuart Pedrell?'

'Nothing. He was a man who never knew how to get the best out of life. A narcissistic sufferer. He suffered for himself. He had a Jewish anxiety. But he was a high-flier in the business world. I knew him as an adolescent, almost as a child. I was a good friend of his father's. The Stuarts set up in Catalonia in the early nineteenth century. They were involved in the hazelnut trade between Reus and London.'

'Where could a man like him have disappeared to, for a whole year, without leaving a single trace?'

'Maybe he enrolled at some foreign university. He'd been getting interested in ecology – he was always getting carried away with some new idea. I once told him: your great advantage over ninety-nine per cent of the population of this country is that you read the *New York Times* every day'. . .

'Do you have any actual evidence that Stuart enrolled at a foreign university?'

'None at all.'

'So?'

'Maybe he went on a trip, but not to the South Seas. Border controls aren't infallible, you know. In fact, I'd say the opposite. A man with an urge to disappear will disappear. Do you know what people were claiming when I went off to the Sacromonte caves? That I had gone to Antarctica with an expedition that I financed. There was even a report in the Movimiento press commenting on the mettle of the Spanish race – that would not be intimidated by the most inaccessible secrets of the world.'

M. Vázquez Montalbán, *Southern Seas* (London: Pluto Press, 1986), pp. 56, 57, 61, 63 and 64.

Notes

[1] J. Colmeiro, 'The Hispanic (dis)connection: some leads and a few missing links', *Journal of Popular Culture*, 34, 3 (2001), 50.
[2] See F. Salgado, 'Manuel Vázquez Montalbán, la formació d'un periodista. (1960–1962): *El Español, Solidaridad Nacional, La Prensa*' (unpublished MA thesis, Universitat Pompeu Fabra, Barcelona, 2005).
[3] *Literatura subnormal* is a concept developed by Vázquez Montalbán in the context of dictatorship to define a kind of avant-garde literature that subverts and parodies traditional forms and genres in order to convey its social critique.
[4] For a much more comprehensive contextualization of the appearance of crime fiction in Spain, one that includes authors who were writing in Spain prior to the *Transición*, see José Rafael Vallés Calatrava, *La novela criminal española* (Granada: Universidad de Granada, 1991), José Colmeiro, *La novela policiaca española: teoría e historia crítica* (Barcelona: Anthropos, 1994) and Patricia Hart, *The Spanish Sleuth: The Detective in Spanish Fiction* (London: Associated University Presses, 1987).
[5] Having been denied, through coercion or consent, in the context of a dictatorship, any sense of citizenship connected to political action, the new urban middle classes created by Francoism were mostly apolitical and focused on defining their identity through consumption.

[6] T. L. Ebert, 'Detecting the phallus: authority, ideology and the production of patriarchal agents in detective fiction', *Rethinking Marxism*, 5, 3 (1992), 6–28.
[7] As studied in José Luis Abellán, *La industria cultural en España* (Madrid: Cuadernos para el diálogo SA, 1975).
[8] Ramón Acín, *Narrativa o consumo literario (1975–1987)* (Zaragoza: Prensas Universitarias, 1990), p. 44; José Rafael Vallés Calatrava, *La novela criminal española* (Granada: Universidad de Granada, 1991), pp. 110–13.
[9] E. Afinoguénova, 'Adorno – a farce character, or: the origins of cultural critique in Spain', in B. Holger and A. Kramer (eds), *In Practice: Adorno, Critical Theory and Cultural Studies* (Oxford: Peter Lang, 2001), p. 185.
[10] Ibid., p. 191.
[11] This has been documented in Ernest Mandel, *Delightful Murder: A Social History of the Crime Story* (Minneapolis: University of Minnesota Press, 1984).
[12] Manuel Vázquez Montalbán, *Southern Seas* (London: Pluto Press, 1986), pp. 76–7.
[13] Further distance from his own endeavour, and the lives and histories of those he is allowed to oversee and have an impact on, is provided by the series' self-reflexivity and critique of the genre. Carvalho attends talks by literary critics on detective fiction and discusses the kind of crime narrative his cases fall under.
[14] For example, in Colmeiro, 'The Hispanic (dis)connection', 54.
[15] From a different point of view – that of Vázquez Montalbán's ability successfully to sustain the writing of a serialized fiction for a long period of time – the design of convincing and connecting secondary characters is certainly crucial. Vázquez Montalbán was not new to such a task, as his highly innovative journalistic work of the late Francoist period and the first years of the transition had included the creation of periodical sections where political commentary was conveyed through the creation of fictional characters and the relationships between them. The most well-known example of this is his 'Capilla Sixtina', the monthly column he published in *Triunfo*, featuring the fictional Sixto Cámara as protagonist, surrounded by a series of secondary characters such as Encarna or Menelao el Aeropagita, as well as other real-life people, in an inextricable mixture of fiction and journalism.
[16] Mari Paz Balibrea, *En La Tierra Baldía: Manuel Vázquez Montalbán y la izquierda española en la postmodernidad* (Barcelona: El Viejo Topo, 1999).
[17] The most important four political parties ranged from the right-wing Alianza Popular (later to become the current Partido Popular) to the Eurocommunist Partido Comunista (later to be integrated in the current Izquierda Unida), and including most importantly the decisive centre-right Unión de Centro Democrático and centre-left Partido Socialista Obrero Español.
[18] Colmeiro, 'The Hispanic (dis)connection', 51.
[19] Vázquez Montalbán, *Southern Seas*, pp. 95–6.

[20] For an extensive analysis of this novel, see M. P. Balibrea, 'Viaje al fin del mundo: política del tiempo y el espacio en *Milenio Carvalho*', in J. F. Colmeiro (ed.), *Manuel Vázquez Montalbán. El compromiso de la memoria* (London: Tamesis, 2007), pp. 197–209.

[21] S. Bayó Belenguer, 'Montalbán's Carvalho series as social critique', in A. Mullen and E. O'Beirne (eds), *Crime Scenes: Detective Narratives in European Culture since 1945* (Amsterdam: Rodopi, 2000), p. 310.

[22] Vázquez Montalbán himself used it in novels outside the Carvalho series, most notably in *El pianista* (1985, The Pianist) and *Galíndez* (1990, Galíndez).

[23] The interest of these novels in exploring the national past is read as a sign of a historicist postmodernism by A. I. Briones García, in 'Novela policiaca española y postmodernismo historicista en los años ochenta', *Anales de la Literatura Española Contemporánea*, 24 (1999), 65–82.

[24] For a more in-depth analysis of these novels see Shelley Godsland and Stewart King, 'Crimes present, motives past: a function of national history in the contemporary Spanish detective novel', *Clues*, 24, 3 (2006), 30–40.

Bibliography

Abellán, J. L., *La industria cultural en España* (Madrid: Cuadernos para el diálogo SA, 1975).

Acín, Ramón, *Narrativa o consumo literario (1975–1987)* (Zaragoza: Prensas Universitarias, 1990).

Afinoguénova, E., 'Adorno – a farce character, or: the origins of cultural critique in Spain', in B. Holger and A. Kramer (eds), *In Practice: Adorno, Critical Theory and Cultural Studies* (Oxford: Peter Lang, 2001), pp.179–92.

Balibrea, Mari Paz, *En la Tierra Baldía: Manuel Vázquez Montalbán y la izquierda española en la postmodernidad* (Barcelona: El Viejo Topo, 1999).

——, 'Viaje al fin del mundo: política del tiempo y el espacio en *Milenio Carvalho*', in J. F. Colmeiro (ed.), *Manuel Vázquez Montalbán. El compromiso de la memoria* (London: Tamesis, 2007), pp. 197–209.

Bayó Belenguer, S., 'Montalbán's Carvalho series as social critique', in A. Mullen and E. O'Beirne (eds), *Crime Scene: Detective Narratives in European Culture since 1945* (Amsterdam: Rodopi, 2000), pp. 300–11.

——, 'Popular collage in the Carvalho series of Manuel Vázquez Montalbán', in S. Godsland and N. Moody (eds), *Reading the Popular in Contemporary Spanish Texts* (Newark: University of Delaware Press, 2004), pp. 26–34.

Briones García, A. I., 'Novela policiaca española y postmodernismo historicista en los años ochenta', *Anales de la Literatura Española Contemporánea*, 24 (1999), 65–82.

Colmeiro, J. F., *La novela policiaca española: teoría e historia crítica* (Barcelona: Anthropos, 1994).

——, 'The Hispanic (dis)connection: some leads and a few missing links', *Journal of Popular Culture*, 34, 3 (2001), 49–64.

Ebert, T. L., 'Detecting the phallus: authority, ideology and the production of patriarchal agents in detective fiction', in *Rethinking Marxism*, 5, 3 (1992), 6–28.

Godsland, S., 'Crimes present, motives past: a function of national history in the contemporary Spanish detective novel', *Clues*, 24, 3 (2006), 30–40.

Hart, P., *The Spanish Sleuth: The Detective in Spanish Fiction* (London: Associated University Presses, 1987).

Mandel, E., *Delightful Murder: A Social History of the Crime Story* (Minneapolis: University of Minnesota Press, 1984).

Salgado, F., *Manuel 'Vázquez Montalbán, la formació d'un periodista (1960–1962), El Español, Solidaridad Nacional, La Prensa'*, unpublished MA thesis, Universitat Pompeu Fabra, Barcelona, 2005.

Santana, M., 'Manuel Vázquez Montalbán's *Los mares del Sur* and the incrimination of the Spanish transition', *Revista de Estudios Hispánicos*, 34 (2000), 535–59.

Vallés Calatrava, José Rafael, *La novela criminal española* (Granada: Universidad de Granada, 1991).

Vázquez Montalbán, M., *Southern Seas* (London: Pluto Press, 1986).

——, *Milenio Carvalho* (two volumes) (Barcelona: Planeta, 2004).

Young, A. R., 'Montalbán's Carvalho: Spanish society, identity, and the detective', in A. Mullen and E. O'Beirne (eds), *Crime Scenes: Detective Narratives in European Culture since 1945* (Amsterdam: Rodopi, 2000), pp. 312–19.

4

Detecting Difference/Constructing Community in Basque, Catalan and Galician Crime Fiction

STEWART KING

Generally, crime fiction in Basque, Catalan and Galician has been treated superficially or entirely ignored by critics. This is because studies on crime fiction from Spain have focused almost exclusively on a limited number of writers, such as Manuel Vázquez Montalbán and Eduardo Mendoza, at the expense of others, thus limiting our understanding of the development of the crime genre in Spain more widely.[1] Furthermore, in the Spanish context the choice of literary language is a significant factor, as authors who write in Basque, Catalan or Galician have received less attention than they perhaps deserve. This chapter, then, seeks to do something to redress this imbalance by providing an introduction to crime fiction in the Basque country, Catalonia and Galicia.

I propose a means of reading national and cultural identities through crime novels by three best-selling authors: Jaume Fuster (1945–98), Carlos G. Reigosa (1948–) and Bernardo Atxaga (1951–). These three authors are important because in their work they use the crime genre to explore issues concerning community in a period of national and cultural regeneration and reconstruction during Spain's transition from a dictatorship to a multicultural democracy. Specifically, through a close reading of Fuster's *Sota el signe de Sagitari* (1986, Under the Sign of Sagittarius), Reigosa's *Crime en Compostela* (1984, Crime in Compostela) and Atxaga's *Gizona bere bakardadean* (1994, The Lone Man), I will examine linguistic identities in Catalonia, the importance of place and socio-cultural transformation in Galicia and, finally, terrorism and the failed imagined community in the Basque country.[2] While the examples are drawn from the Basque, Catalan and Galician contexts, this chapter goes beyond the specific examples provided to offer a means of reading nationhood in crime fiction.

Imagining crime and imagined communities

The link between national identity and fiction is one that is strongly argued in Benedict Anderson's landmark study of nationalism, *Imagined Communities*, in which he suggests that an awareness of the nation came into existence with the development of mass print culture associated with capitalist modernity – specifically realist literature and newspapers – in the eighteenth and nineteenth centuries. For Anderson, fiction and the print media enabled nations to be 'imagined', as readers began to identify the fictional world of the novel with the 'real' world in which they lived. In Anderson's analysis, the citizens of a nation or the members of a cultural group identify with a specific social space through the constant repetition of images and ideas which are easily recognizable to them. These images help to develop 'deep, horizontal comradeship with others', which, in turn, distinguishes the members of one nation from those of another.[3]

While for Anderson the birth of this national imagining occurs at very particular moments in a nation's past, specifically in the eighteenth and nineteenth centuries, it is important, nevertheless, to examine how the contemporary nation is reproduced in fiction and film and modern media, such as television, radio and the Internet. Crime narratives are especially suited to this task of imagining nationhood because they are fundamentally concerned with the very issues of community and transgression. For criminologist Alison Young, community is not just imagined through identifications between real and fictional worlds, but through crime itself. She argues that: 'In criminal justice policy, in criminological theory and in the practices of criminal law can be found, first, an imagined community; second, an identifiable subject which represents a threat to the community; third, a desire to inflict violence upon that subject in the name of the community.'[4] Young believes that the community identifies with the victim, as all members of the community are potential victims at the hands of the criminal. This community, she argues, is a fiction: 'a nostalgic desire for oneness and unity' which structures itself 'around its dependence upon fear, alienation and separateness for its elements to make sense'. Thus the criminal is an essential element which must be 'sacrificed in order to maintain a fragile community'.[5]

Young's observations are not limited to the representation of real criminal acts and cases in any given society. They are equally valid for fictional crime stories, which she examines in a chapter of her study *Imagining Crime: Textual Outlaws and Criminal Conversations*. Like crime itself, crime fiction is fundamentally concerned with constructing community. In the genre, community is established through the investigative process in which individuals – usually suspects – are seen to be connected to each other through their relationship with the victim and possibly the criminal.

The role of a detective is crucial to the creation of these fictional communities. For the uncomprehending reader in search of an explanation behind the crime, the detective mediates the physical, social and cultural world represented in the text; he or she guides readers 'through uncharted areas of modern society', helping them to understand the world in which they live.[6] Readers of crime fiction, then, are 'encouraged to identify with the detective and to share the detective's worldview', creating in the reader an imaginary interlocutor.[7]

This connection between reader and detective, whether policeman, private eye or an individual caught up in a mystery or problem which they must resolve, is further strengthened by the development of identity politics which has taken place in the West since the late 1970s and early 1980s, and which in crime fiction saw the creation of a new breed of detective – often one who came from what was previously seen as a marginal group including women, gay and lesbian people, or black, gypsy and other ethnic minorities. The importance of detective protagonists associated with particular groups or communities is that they present readers with any number of the possible identities with which they may identify.[8]

This is the case with fictional Basque, Catalan and Galician detectives. In crime novels written on Spain's cultural periphery a specific national subject position is constructed through the reader's identification with a Basque-, Catalan- or Galician-speaking protagonist whose crime solving within a particular geographic space – the Basque country, Catalonia or Galicia – serves to define the symbolic boundaries of the nation.

Crime fictions in the Basque country, Catalonia and Galicia are, thus, more than mere light entertainment. Indeed, in these regions they are intricately linked to cultural survival and regeneration. They are a privileged site in which writers have sought to develop a sense of shared nationhood and shared language as a means of resisting a broader Spanish imagined community which had been promoted by the regime headed by Francisco Franco. To appreciate fully the role and function of crime fiction in these regions, it is necessary to have some understanding of the cultural policies and practices enacted since the Spanish Civil War (1936–9).

The Franco regime (1939–75) was obsessed with the political, cultural and linguistic unity of the Spanish state, an obsession that led to the imposition over the entire country of a single understanding of Spanish national identity based almost exclusively on Castilian language and culture. As a result, Spain's minority cultures were subjected to a process of Castilianization, as the public and private use – written or oral – of Basque, Catalan and Galician was proscribed by law, in 1937, 1938 and 1939 respectively, and the teaching of these languages was banned. Baptismal and place names were Castilianized, thereby assuring a Castilian identity for the physical landscape and the people who lived there. Transgressors were fined and often physically abused, and prominent cultural and political figures from these regions were either forced into exile or suffered imprisonment and even death. In universities, Basque, Catalan and Galician studies were discontinued. Books and print media in these languages were burned or pulped, and censorship ensured that few books were published. During the 1940s, for example, only thirty books were published in Basque, half of which were religious. Catalan fared better with fifty-three titles alone published in 1947 (up from four in 1944), while only three works in Galician were published between 1939 and 1947.[9] Translation of foreign – that is, non-Spanish – literature into minority languages was prohibited until 1962, when censorship laws were relaxed slightly.[10]

Franco's aim to make Castilian the vernacular throughout the country was further aided by the post-war mass migration of unskilled, Castilian-speaking workers and their families from other parts of Spain to the Basque country and Catalonia. This migration led to a substantial increase in the number of monolingual Castilian speakers in these regions. In Catalonia, for example, by 1975 barely half the population used Catalan as their regular language of communication.[11] In the Basque country the percentage of Basque speakers was even lower. In the early 1990s only 25 per cent of the 2.5 million inhabitants of the Autonomous Basque Community could claim to speak the language.[12] The situation in Galicia was different, however. A region beset by chronic poverty and lack of economic opportunities, Galicia has traditionally produced migrants rather than attract them. As a result, it is estimated that approximately 90 per cent of the three million people residing in Galicia speak the language.[13]

The Franco regime was ultimately unsuccessful in its bid to eradicate Spain's minority languages and cultures and replace them with a single 'Spanish' identity. Within three years of the dictator's death in 1975

Spaniards overwhelmingly approved a constitution which effectively buried the Francoist vision of a country unified politically, culturally and linguistically. The centralized state was partially dismantled as Spain was divided into seventeen different political and administrative autonomous regions which are responsible for education, health, social services and culture.[14] In addition, the constitution recognized Spain's diverse cultural and linguistic heritage. For example, in article 3.1 Castilian – and not 'Spanish' – was confirmed as the official language of the state, while article 3.2 recognized Basque, Catalan and Galician as also being Spanish languages, granting them an official status within their respective communities.[15]

Following the approval of the constitution, one of the earliest tasks of the Basque, Catalan and Galician autonomous governments was to set in train a series of linguistic and cultural measures designed to redress the history of neglect and repression at the hands of the central government. Their aim was to reconstruct a community based upon a shared language and culture. This is clearly expressed in the Language Normalization Act for Catalonia (1983), which states that,

> The restoration of Catalan to its rightful place as Catalonia's own language is the unquestionable right and duty of the Catalan people and must be respected and protected. In this regard, knowledge of the language must spread throughout the whole of Catalan society, to all citizens regardless of the language they normally speak, within a global framework in which everyone will accept the use of both languages [Castilian and Catalan] and recognise and contribute to the recovery of Catalan as one of the fundamental aspects of the reconstruction of Catalonia.[16]

Similar linguistic policies advancing Basque and Galician were also implemented in their respective communities following the passing of the Basque Decreto de Bilingüismo y la Ley de Normalización Lingüística (1982) and the Galician Lei de normalización lingüística de Galicia (1983).

These laws, together with the reinstatement of Basque, Catalan and Galician in schools and universities, the establishment of television, radio and print media in these languages and financial subsidies for the arts led to a cultural renaissance in the Basque country, Catalonia and Galicia. The extent of this boom can be seen in the remarkable development of publishing in minority languages after Franco's death. The number of titles published annually in Galician rose from a mere 78 to 1,148 between 1972 and 1995, while in Basque there was a tenfold increase from 95 titles published in 1976 to 968 in 1995. In Catalonia, where the publishing industry was already relatively strong, 5,791 titles were published in 1995, up from approximately 800 in 1976.[17]

Freed from censorship restrictions, publishers reprinted works by major writers which had been poorly distributed during the dictatorship, while new authors experimented with literary forms, particularly popular genres, such as crime, erotica, romance, horror and science fictions, children's literature and even westerns. The aim of this so-called 'mass' literature was to popularize reading among a predominantly young sector of a society which was increasingly educated in Basque, Catalan and Galician and to attract readers who had previously read in Castilian.

Catalan crime fiction: investigating language and identity

In comparison with other national literatures, the development and acceptance of crime fiction in Catalan culture has been slow and is a relatively recent phenomenon. The genre entered Catalan culture via translations of Conan Doyle's Sherlock Holmes stories in the first decade of the twentieth century.[18] However, the first known crime novel written directly in Catalan – *La meva mort* (My Death) by M. Poal-Aregall – was published only in 1924. Other writers followed Poal-Aregall's example, but the outbreak of war in 1936 and the subsequent repression of Catalan culture by the Franco regime hindered the genre's development. While individual writers, such as Rafael Tasis, Manuel de Pedrolo and Maria-Aurèlia Capmany, were able to publish well-received crime novels in Catalan during the 1950s and 1960s, they had little impact on Catalan literary culture, as the majority of writers were more concerned with producing works of high culture in order to prove that Catalan was a language worthy of literature.[19]

The first serious and sustained attempt to introduce the genre into Catalan culture began in 1963 with the establishment of the Cua de Palla, a series of crime novels chosen by Pedrolo, who aimed to foster a Catalan-language-reading public through popular forms. The series, which consisted mainly of crime novels translated from English and French, was not a commercial success and publication ceased in 1970.[20] Despite being a commercial failure, the Cua de Palla series did, however, forge a literary language on which later writers would draw to produce their own fictions.[21]

Pedrolo's desire for an autochthonous crime fiction with a substantial number of readers was finally realized in the 1970s and 1980s, as numerous authors, such as Jaume Fuster, Andreu Martín, Margarida Aritzeta, Josep-Maria Palau i Camps, the Mallorcan writers Maria-Antònia Oliver and Antoni Serra, and Valencian authors Ferran Torrent and Josep Lluís Seguí experimented with the genre, producing a boom in crime narratives.

The genre's success in Catalonia can be attributed primarily to the efforts of Jaume Fuster, a Barcelonan writer and critic, whose crime novels and short stories, including *De mica en mica s'omple la pica* (1972, Little by Little the Basin Fills), *Les claus de vidre* (1984, The Glass Keys) and *Sota el signe de Sagitari* (1986), quickly became best-sellers.[22] Fuster was a major promoter of genre fiction. In addition to crime novels, he wrote a Tolkeinesque trilogy set in the Mediterranean – *L'illa de les Tres Taronges* (1983, The Island of the Three Oranges), *L'anell de ferro* (1985, The Iron Ring) and *El jardí de les palmeres* (1993, The Garden of Palm Trees). He was also an active member of a writing collective that published collaborative erotic, science, horror and detective fictions under the pseudonym Ofèlia Dracs. The aim of this collective, according to one of its members, Maria-Antònia Oliver, was to write 'popular' fictions that would resonate with the Catalan reading public so that 'readers did not have to go to translations or to Spanish books to get what their own culture was not offering them'.[23]

Fuster's *Sota el signe de Sagitari* is a perfect example of a fiction that resonates with the public. The detective at the centre of the novel is Lluís Arquer – Lew Archer – Fuster's homage to Ross McDonald. Arquer first appeared in a series of short stories in the weekly current affairs and cultural magazine, *El món*, in 1982 and 1983. A year later, in 1984, seventeen stories were expanded and published in a collection that has enjoyed great popularity with twelve reprints by 1996. Just as Hollywood had been drawn to the hard-boiled crime genre as a source of film scripts, Catalan Television (TV3) made thirteen stories into a television series of the same name, of which only nine were screened in 1986, the same year that Arquer returned in *Sota el signe de Sagitari*, a fully fledged novel in the hard-boiled tradition.

Sota el signe de Sagitari begins with a relatively simple mystery. A prominent public figure in the newly reinstated Catalan government employs Arquer to find his missing son, Jaume, a 27-year-old who has been caught up in radical politics. Arquer's investigation, however, quickly becomes complicated as he discovers an international drug-smuggling ring and corrupt police. Furthermore, he is witness to multiple murders and throughout the novel he is deceived, manipulated, beaten, kidnapped, forcibly given heroin and tortured. He also falls in and out of love.

By the end of the novel Arquer has exposed a plot by right-wing Spanish nationalists to import and distribute drugs in the Basque country with the aim of undermining community cohesion in order to minimize the threat posed by Basque nationalism to the Spanish state. They are aided in this task by the mafia, unscrupulous public figures, such as Arquer's employer, and police officers. Despite providing the authorities with the necessary proof, Arquer cannot convince the national police and Civil Guard to investigate further. They whitewash the investigation by limiting it to drug smuggling, and hence erase any link with state involvement in criminal activities.

The events investigated in *Sota el signe de Sagitari* are not limited to Catalonia. Indeed, the different locations to which Arquer travels in the novel – Palma de Mallorca, Naples, New York and San Sebastián – read like the outlets of an international fashion designer. However, despite its international scope, *Sota el signe de Sagitari* is firmly grounded in Catalan society and culture and Arquer presents a Catalan understanding of the world, central to which is the link between language and cultural identity.

Recognition of the importance of the relationship between language and crime fiction to articulate a particular national identity is not new. Dennis Porter argues that the North American hard-boiled novel, on which many Catalan writers drew when writing their own fictions, was in part an act of 'cultural and linguistic rebellion similar to the one that had already been completed in the political sphere'.[24] According to Porter, through the fast-talking, wise-cracking gumshoe, American writers sought to represent a 'native American idiom' distinct from British English.[25] While in the Catalan context a similar process can be achieved by the simple act of writing in Catalan, rather than Castilian, to do so, nevertheless, is to mark out a separate Catalan cultural and linguistic space.

It is worth noting here the importance given to linguistic clues within the novel. Arquer is hyper-sensitive to language variation. He notes, for example, how Castilian-speaking policemen mangle Catalan words – 'Txeneralità', instead of 'Generalitat', for example – and he is particularly attentive to accent: a barman speaks an 'andalús tancat' (with a strong Andalusian accent), an Englishwoman speaks a Castilian '*d'allende los mares*' (from over the seas, that is, a Latin American form of Spanish), a Latin American thug has the 'accent de cantador de tangos' (accent of a tango singer), while a Barcelonan thug speaks 'un castellà xava de la Barceloneta' (the lower-class Castilian spoken in the port area of Barcelona) and the Spanish consul in Naples converses in 'un castellà engolat, de funcionari de primera' (a throaty Castilian of a first-class civil servant).[26] Arquer also identifies the mere hint of a Galician accent in a Civil Guard colonel's speech and, despite scant knowledge of English, in a scene reminiscent of Sherlock Holmes, Arquer can even detect 'ecos de sirtaki, perfums de retsina i brises d'un Egeu remot' (echoes of sirtaki, the smell of retsina and the breeze from the far off Aegean) in the English spoken by a Greek-American FBI agent.[27]

Arquer's particular attention to language and accent is significant, as it can be read as representative of a Catalan understanding of cultural identity by which who you are is determined, largely, by what and how you speak. Language and accent are, thus, markers of cultural difference. Although Barcelona and Catalonia are bilingual, the dominant language of the narrative is Catalan. It is the language through which the narrative is retold and it is also the language into which the other languages are translated. It is 'normalized' in line with the Generalitat's policy of making Catalan the main language of verbal and written interaction in Catalonia.

The centrality of Catalan and the representation of other languages are important in bilingual cultural and linguistic contexts, such as Catalonia. Castilian, when it is not simply translated into Catalan, is represented textually in italics, thus marking it as different, other. Although it is a language of daily communication in Catalonia, Castilian's strangeness is no different from that of any other language, such as English, Italian and Basque, which also appear italicized throughout the novel.

The foreignness of Castilian is further emphasized in a passage set in JFK airport in New York where Arquer manages to convince an Iberia Airlines official to allow him to enter a restricted area. He surmises that his success is probably due to 'el fet de parlar-li la seva llengua i la solidesa de la història' (the fact that I spoke her language [i.e. Castilian] and the strength of my story).[28] This use of the possessive – la seva (her) – is significant. Although Arquer speaks Castilian, it is not his language. The use of possessives to denote national belonging is reinforced throughout the novel when representatives of the Spanish state – politicians, bureaucrats, police officers – refer to Spain as 'el nostre país' (our country).[29] Arquer's country, in contrast, is clearly Barcelona or Catalonia.[30]

Arquer's relationship with a specific cultural and linguistic – national – space is repeated in numerous other Catalan crime novels, but it is not a phenomenon limited to Catalonia. As I will demonstrate in the following section, the link between detective and place also plays an important role in Galician crime narratives.

Galician crime fiction: place and stereotypes

In comparison with Catalan literature, crime fiction in Galician appeared quite late; critics generally point to Carlos G. Reigosa's *Crime en Compostela*, published in 1984, as the foundational text of Galician detective fiction. An author of non-genre fiction and a journalist, Carlos Reigosa (born in Lagoa de Pastoriza, 1948) has, to date, published four crime novels: *Crime en Compostela*, *O misterio do barco perdido* (1988, The Mystery of the Lost Boat), *A guerra do tabaco* (1996, The Tobacco War) and *Narcos* (2001, Narcos), all of which have received considerable attention and all of which have been translated into Castilian and even Catalan. Following Reigosa, other Galician writers also produced detective novels, including Pepe Carballude, Manuel Forcadela, Suso de Toro and, more recently, Domingo Villar, with *Investigación 091* (1989, Investigation 091), *Sangue sobre a neve* (1990, Blood on the Snow), *Ambulancia* (1990, Ambulance) and *Ollos de auga* (2006, Water-Blue Eyes) respectively. None, with the possible exception of Domingo Villar, has enjoyed the same success as Reigosa.[31]

Crime en Compostela tells the story of Nivardo Castro, a private investigator, who is employed to solve the mystery surrounding the murder of a Compostelan businessman, Aurelio Xieiro. Like many of his compatriots, Castro does not live in Galicia, as he was forced to emigrate because of poverty, first to Germany, then to north Africa where he completed his military service and later to New York where he trained as a private investigator before moving to Madrid, where he works in the Spanish office of Stevenson and Co., an international detective and protection agency. As a result of the long period he has spent outside his homeland, Castro does not see himself as Galician, preferring to describe himself as an 'aventureiro internacional' (international adventurer).[32]

Place is central to the construction of cultural identities in the novel, and it is significant that the narrative opens with Castro travelling on a plane between Madrid and Santiago. For Castro, Santiago represents 'a cidade galega internacional por antonomasia' (the Galician city par excellence).[33] Thus, the saintly city not only functions as the background where the crime and its resolution are acted out, but also plays an important role in the narrative, becoming symbolic of Galician cultural difference. Nationalism, Anthony Smith argues, is predicated on the notion that nations have definite boundaries which clearly separate members of one nation from another.[34] In *Crime en Compostela*, Nivardo articulates these differences by contrasting Santiago de Compostela with other cities, particularly Madrid. It is significant, for example, that Madrid is almost always associated with foreign – that is, non-Spanish – cities. For Castro, his international experience counts for naught because he believes that the crime cannot be resolved in the same way as if it had occurred 'en Madrid, en París ou en Miami' (in Madrid, in Paris or in Miami).[35] Nevertheless, his extensive international experience does empower him to make comparisons between the Spanish and Galician capitals which – in the reader's mind – further reinforce the cultural borders between the two nations. For example, in his discussion of student life in Santiago, Castro sees Madrid as having more in common with Paris than with Santiago. Although this may seem a superficial comparison, Castro is convinced that in Santiago 'todo tiña que ser – que suceder– doutra maneira, con outro ritmo' (everything has to be different, to happen differently, with another rhythm) to the rest of the world.[36]

By juxtaposing the act (crime) with the city (Compostela), the title suggests that the Galician capital is just as important to the development of the plot as the discovery of the murderer's identity. This link is further highlighted at the beginning of the novel when his journalist friend, Carlos Conde, states that if Castro is to discover the identity of Aurelio's killer he must decipher the mystery of the city itself. Conde explains to Castro that 'iso que tes aí diante non é soamente unha cidade, é todo un sistema filosófico e relixioso . . . gardado polo misterio' (what you have in front of you is not only a city, it is an entire philosophical and religious system . . . shrouded in mystery) and the detective is so fascinated by this second mystery that he decides that 'ademais de investigar aquel crime compostelán . . . adicaría unha parte do seu tempo a coñecer aquela cidade da que tantas referencias tiña e da que, sen embargo, tan poucas cousas sabía' (in addition to investigating the Compostelan crime . . . he would dedicate a part of his time there to getting to know that city about which so much was said, but about which he knew so little).[37]

Castro's ability to solve the case, however, is hampered by the stereotypical images he has of Galicia. These are expressed when he visits the Museo do Pobo Galego (Museum of the Galician People), which Castro is surprised to find is housed in an opulent seventeenth-century building. For Castro, it 'debería estar en calquera sitio, menos alí; quizabes nunha brava encosta ou nun ermo outeiro de Melide, Palas de Rei ou Monterroso, no centro de Galicia . . . rodeadas de espacio natural por todas partes' (should be in any other place, but there. Perhaps on a wild coast or on a hill deep in Melide, Palas de Rei o Monterroso, in the centre of Galicia . . . surrounded entirely by nature).[38] Castro sees Galicia as a country of pre-modern rural traditions and superstitions in which the Galician people do not belong to urban centres or modernity, but to an idealized image of an ageless and static countryside. This image of Galicia, he goes on to realize – if uncritically – is based on the novels of Wenceslao Fernández Flórez, a Galician author whose work forms part of a Castilian-language ruralist tradition which has helped perpetuate the image of Galicia as a place largely untouched by modernity.[39]

In contrast to the clichéd images Castro has of Galicia, he soon discovers that the sleepy, mysterious backwater he has imagined is currently gripped by capitalist fever. In contrasting these different images, Reigosa does not seek simply to replace an outmoded image of Galicia with a current one. Rather, the two images exist constantly in tension, as can be seen in Carlos Conde's statement that Santiago de Compostela – and by extension Galicia – 'é, en moitos aspectos, unha poboación que, condanada á modernidade, resístese a abandonalas súas formas de vida e de relación social tradicionais' (is, in many ways, a place that, condemned to modernity, still refuses to abandon its traditional social relations and way of life).[40] This tension between past and present, tradition and modernity is a constant feature of *Crime en Compostela* and other novels of the 1980s, as many writers sought to present a new image of Galicia.[41] We can see the simultaneous existence of past and present in Castro's descriptions of the Praza del Obradoiro (Obradoiro Square) in the heart of the medieval quarter: 'o románico arcaizante da portada do Colexio de San Xerome – hoxe Rectorado da Universidade –, o barroco exuberante e curviliño da fachada da Catedral, o plateresco requintado de gótico do Hospital Real – agora Hostal de cinco estrelas –' (the archaic romanesque features of the Colexio de San Xerome doorway which these days houses the vice-chancellor's offices, the cathedral's exuberant and curved facade, the plateresque Gothic features of the Royal Hospital, now a five-star hotel).[42] Although these buildings have retained their original names, their function has undergone a profound transformation in light of current necessities. Furthermore, the use of temporal markers such as 'hoxe' (today) and 'agora' (now) suggest the current functions of the buildings are not permanent, but that they are, like all cultural products and identities, constantly subject to change. These buildings can thus be read as traditional representations of Galicia which have been updated in order to correspond to contemporary realities.

This contrast between old and new visions of Galicia is clearly represented in the attitudes towards Galician society and culture expressed by the novel's two main characters – Castro and his journalist friend, Carlos Conde. Unlike the Madrid-based detective, Conde lives in Santiago and he has a more realistic understanding of Galician society than his friend. In fact, Conde is interested more in what the case potentially says about contemporary Galicia than in catching the killer. For Conde, who plans to write several newspaper and magazine articles on the topic, the investigation offers him an opportunity to

> poñer esta cidade coas patas para riba e converterse nun guía que, no canto de amosar Compostela e a súa arte impoñente, ensina as miserias e sordideces daqueles que viven á conta dela e da fe e das necesidades dos que veñen aquí, xa sexa para rezar, para estudiar, para que os vexa un médico ou para descansar. Porque Compostela, xa o comprobarás, ten as dúas caras. Pero os guías turísticos soamente falan dunha delas.[43]

> (turn this city upside-down and to become a guide that, rather than sing his love of Compostela and its imposing art, shows the misery and sordid side of those that live there and the faith and needs of those that come here to pray, to study, to see a doctor or to rest. Because Compostela, as you will see, has two faces, but the tourist guides only speak about one of them.)

Given that Conde writes an article entitled 'Crime en Compostela', we can perhaps interpret the figure of the journalist as the alter ego of the author. In light of this, the above quote can be read as the motive behind the author's use of the detective story: his desire to challenge the ruralist stereotype of Galicia, peddled by writers such as Fernández Flórez and accepted by Castro, by juxtaposing these stereotypes with a modern city in which illegal business deals, corruption, changing sexual mores, prostitution and murder coexist. Reigosa, thus, situates his novel within a broader Galician cultural movement that, since the death of Franco, has sought to question the validity and to challenge the ongoing influence of such representations of Galician identity and culture.

Basque crime fiction: questioning nationalism

With only 700,000 potential readers, Basque is the most precarious of the three minority languages examined in this chapter. This relatively small reading public has had profound implications for the type of literature produced by Basque authors, for whom the traditional division between elite and popular culture is not relevant, as the publishing industry is too small to justify specialist series dedicated to popular fictions such as those that exist in Catalan and Galician.[44] For Javier Cillero Goiriastuena, the collapse of the elite–popular division in the Basque context has meant that writers have greater freedom to experiment with literary genre and style. One such example is Bernardo Atxaga, pseudonym of Joseba Irazu Garmendia, who is one of the few authors writing in Basque who can live by his writing. Atxaga has published over sixteen novels, short-story and poetry collections. His work ranges from popular children's fiction to elite postmodernist high culture, such as *Obabakoak* (1988, Obabakoak), which was the first novel in Basque to win Spain's National Literature Prize (for literature written in any of Spain's official languages). Many of Atxaga's works have been translated into Castilian and other languages. *Obabakoak* alone has been translated into over twenty languages.

Like the Catalan and Galician cases, Basque literature in general is seen as serving a civic, nation-building function: to represent the nation and the identity of the Basques who reside there.[45] According to Cillero Goiriastuena, crime fiction in Basque, especially in the 1980s, largely conformed to this function, as writers created:

> un arquetipo de detective o investigador aficionado en algunos casos en el que abundaban los siguientes rasgos: era un hombre cercano a la cuarentena de años, hablaba perfectamente euskera y destacaba por sus actividades de apoyo al idioma vasco, mostraba un rechazo consciente o inconsciente para con la burguesía vasca, e impulsaba varios símbolos de identidad vascos, como la ikurriña o bandera vasca, etc. En algunos casos se mostraba crítico con la inmigración llegada de España, si bien de manera solapada, y trataba de encontrar una especie de paraíso perdido en el campo vasco y en los campesinos o baserritarras, a quienes consideraba guardianes de las tradiciones vascas.[46]

> (an archetype of the detective or in some cases amateur sleuth who share the following characteristics: he is a man of approximately forty years of age who speaks perfect Basque and who stands out for his active support for the Basque language. He rejects consciously or unconsciously the Basque bourgeoisie and is motivated by various symbols of Basque iden-

tity, such as the ikurriña or Basque flag, and so forth. At times he is critical of Spanish immigration, if only surreptitiously, and he tries to find a sort of paradise lost in the Basque countryside and in the farmers, or baserritarras, whom he considers guardians of Basque traditions.)

Nevertheless, in the 1990s a more critical approach to nationalism appeared in Basque crime fiction in the works of Itxaro Borda, Jon Alonso and Harkaitz Cano.[47] This critical approach to Basque nationalism can be seen in Bernardo Atxaga's *Gizona bere bakardadean* (1994), which was translated into Castilian as *El hombre solo* (The Lone Man) by Arantza Sabán and the author himself.

El hombre solo is a psychological thriller that tells the story of a man 'al que todos llamaban Carlos' (known to everyone as Carlos).[48] An ex-member of the Basque terrorist organization, ETA, Carlos now runs a hotel on the outskirts of Barcelona with two other ex-militants, Guiomar and Ugarte, as well as Ugarte's wife, Laura, and their 5-year-old son, Pascal. Although not related, they form a sort of family based on their shared activist past. The family, however, is threatened when Carlos, without his friends' knowledge, decides to shelter two fugitive members of ETA (*etarras*) who, having assassinated a Spanish army colonel, are on the run from the police.[49]

The story takes place over five days between 28 June and 2 July 1982 during the football World Cup hosted by Spain. This event is important because Carlos's attempts to help the two fugitives escape are hampered, initially, by the police security for the Polish national team which is staying at the hotel and, later, following a tip from someone inside the hotel, by anti-terrorist police posing as a journalist and camera crew. The narrative tension, which increases as the novel progresses, hinges on whether Carlos can assist the two *etarras* to escape the police, without the police being able to prove that the fugitives were ever in the hotel.

Even though *El hombre solo* is set in Barcelona, it can be read as a profound interrogation of the divisions in contemporary Basque society. Rather than diminish the connection to the Basque country, the distance actually intensifies it, as seen in Carlos's observation that in 'exile' he is more conscious of all things Basque, particularly surnames.[50] The intensity is focused on the figure of Carlos and it is through Carlos that Atxaga provides a critique of radical nationalism.

Carlos cuts a sympathetic, if contradictory, figure. His story is, in his own words, similar to that of many Basques during the Franco regime in that it involved being detained at a police station or jailed.[51] Politicized by the perceived repression of Basque culture and identity by the regime, Carlos joined ETA in the late 1960s when the organization first resorted to violence. Since then, over eight hundred deaths have resulted from bombings, assassinations, deaths in custody, kidnappings and state-sanctioned anti-terrorist groups. Carlos was a member for ten years, during which he was involved in several actions, including the kidnapping of a Basque businessman, whom he later murdered. For this, he spent four years in jail until he was released in 1977 as part of an amnesty for political prisoners that was negotiated following the death of Franco.[52] While ETA's opposition to the dictatorship initially gained it substantial supporters not only from among Basque nationalists, but also from among those opposed to the regime, ETA has now divided Basque society. The indiscriminate bombings as well as the kidnappings and assassinations, such as the fictional ones carried out by Carlos, have led to a marked decrease in support for ETA, even within the Basque country, where large demonstrations rejecting violence have been held over the last decade.

Like many Basques, Carlos no longer believes that the armed struggle provides a credible solution to the problems facing the Basque country. He finds the organization's ideals 'una simpleza y una caricatura de análisis político' (simplistic and a caricature of political analysis) and he has a heated debate with Jone, one of the *etarras* hiding in the hotel's bakery, which leads him to state clearly that he no longer identifies with the organization.[53] The decision by Carlos and the others at the hotel to reject ETA, the fact that they feel that they can no longer live in the Basque country and Carlos's criticisms of the organization's motives, rhetoric and actions demonstrate the failure of radical nationalism to unite Basques under a common banner. Instead of unity, Basque society is profoundly divided and Atxaga represents this division in the lone man of the title, Carlos.

While real or fictional supporters of ETA are rarely framed in a positive light, Carlos elicits some sympathy from readers. Rather than rejecting Carlos because of his actions, readers come to see the world through his perspective. The narrative is told primarily from Carlos's point of view, which enables readers to see the contradictory impulses which led him to hide the fugitives. Nevertheless, Carlos's point of view is not entirely coherent. He hears other voices, from the 'Rata' (Rat), his conscience which criticizes his actions and the motivations behind the decision to hide the *etarras*, to 'Sabino', his old mentor, whose voice advises Carlos how to act in the face of danger. Other voices also appear, such as his brother's and the vengeful voice of the widow of the businessman whom Carlos had kidnapped and later killed. These voices limit the readers' capacity to identify with Carlos's world-view and they also highlight that no single point of view can represent the diverse voices that make up Basque society.

El hombre solo is ultimately about the failure of grand narratives, such as nationalism and socialism, to create cohesive societies.[54] More than recounting failure however, Atxaga uses the novel to demonstrate emphatically the destructive nature of radical nationalism. This can be seen in the tragic conclusion to the novel when Carlos's attempt to create a diversion by lighting a bushfire so that the two *etarras* can escape the police cordon literally backfires. While the two *etarras* are able to get away, a change in the wind turns the fire towards an area where the 5-year-old Pascal normally plays, and he dies. Unable at first to face the consequences of his actions, and with his head exploding with a cacophony of accusatory voices, Carlos strips and attempts to drown himself in a natural pool called La Banyera. Nevertheless, the Rata's insistence that he is a coward spurs him to leave the dangerous waters but, before he can act, he is shot by a policeman from the anti-terrorist squad and he dies, naked and alone, in the water. Although he has tried to escape the influence of ETA, Carlos's decision to help the two militants ultimately proves fatal. The community he had established with Guiomar, Ugarte, Laura and Pascal is destroyed by Carlos's renewed association with radical nationalism. *El hombre solo* can thus be read as a warning. Pascal's death demonstrates that even tacit support for violent radical nationalists is potentially destructive not only for individuals but also for community cohesion.

Conclusion

With its focus on community and transgression, the crime genre is an ideal site for investigating issues pertinent to the nation and to the shaping of national and cultural identities. In this sense, crime fictions in Spain's minority languages are not just escapist literature. Instead, they form part of a broader cultural project to rediscover, recreate and reproduce distinct Basque, Catalan and Galician nations following the decentring of Spanish nationhood which has taken place since Franco's death in 1975. While the aim may be to narrate an independent national space, the three novels examined in this chapter clearly demonstrate that the broader Spanish nation-state is a constant referent which cannot be easily ignored or rejected. In *Sota el signe de Sagitari*, although for Lluís Arquer it may be clear that he is Catalan and not Spanish, his interaction with the Iberia Airlines official in New York is successful precisely because she takes him to be her compatriot, that is, a fellow Spaniard. And, in fact, it can be argued that in their exchange Arquer deliberately takes advantage of the ambiguity of being a citizen of a larger nation-state. In *Sota el signe de Sagitari* as well as in *Crime en Compostela* and *El hombre solo* it is clear that the Basque country, Catalonia and Galicia exist within an asymmetrical relationship with a larger national body – Spain, as a result of which the Basque, Catalan and Galician communities represented in these novels are overshadowed by a broadly defined Spanish community. While shared features can be identified in each of the three works, these novels underscore, however, that there is no single approach to imagining the nation in crime fiction. Arquer is a confident member of the Catalan-speaking community with which he clearly identifies; Nivardo Castro, on the other hand, begins to grasp the significance of what it may mean to be Galician only towards the end of the novel, while Atxaga's anti-hero, Carlos, is representative of a deeply fractured society. Regardless of whether fully formed or failed communities are represented, crime fictions from the Basque country, Catalonia and Galicia investigate and interrogate the limits of national identity.

* * *

Extracts from *El hombre solo* (The Lone Man) by Bernardo Atxaga, trans. Margaret Jull Costa

In the previous scene Carlos, the protagonist, has realized that his plan to give shelter to the two ETA operatives is in danger of being discovered. This moment marks the beginning of the thriller in many ways, as he has to get the two etarras *out of the hotel before the police and his colleagues and the friends at the hotel discover them.*

Carlos walked on down to the bakery silently cursing. Neptune, who brought them their fish – and who, as Ugarte had quite rightly suspected, had also brought Jon and Jone – was just the sort of person that Sabino had warned him against. Sooner or later, Neptune would give himself away, even more obviously than he had to Ugarte. What was happening wasn't Neptune's fault though, because, as Sabino also used to say, to people of limited intelligence you give only limited responsibility; no, it was his fault, for taking on something that Neptune had agreed to do on his behalf. Neptune had said to him: 'If we don't help them, the police will just swat them like flies on a wall.' He had said: 'How long would we have to hide them at the hotel?' Neptune: 'A week at most. As soon as things quieten down a bit in Bilbao, I'll put them in the truck and take them back, as quietly as a fox stealing chickens.' And he had said: 'In that case, fine. It'll be like old times, a week of excitement.'

Carlos swore again. He had shown a complete lack of imagination; he was behaving like one of those people who only learn through painful personal experience. Besides, fancy using phrases like that. *It'll be like old times, a week of excitement.* It was ridiculous. It was a joke. Those words would cost him very dear. Four years in prison for collaborating with armed activists, and considerably more than that if Ugarte's fears were well-founded and the bank raids of five or six years back came to light. Yes, all of that could so easily happen. 'God doesn't work miracles for armed activists, and anyone who fails to act prudently or who doesn't observe the security rules is done for,' Sabino used to say. And it was true. In his case too, things had begun to go wrong: instead of the agreed week, Jon and Jone had been there nearly two. If Neptune didn't take them with him the following Sunday, it would be nearly three. However you looked at it, that was too long. Pascal had seen the gun and Pascal's father – was he the only one? – had begun to suspect that something was going on.

He saw the supper trays as soon as he turned on the light in the bakery, one of them was empty, with just a few crumbs on it, the food on the other tray was almost untouched. On that second tray – Carlos thought it was probably Jone's – lay a crudely printed sheet of paper. The pamphlet was entitled 'This democracy is nothing but a façade' and it appeared to be a summary of the ideas being put forward by the organization at the time. He put it in his shirt pocket and shared out the leftover food on the trays between the plates. A minute later, he was opening the door of the storehouse and preparing to be greeted by his dogs. (pp. 48–9)

. . .

The next scene provides the reader with insight into Carlos's solitary nature. The reader is also introduced to Donata, the interpreter for the Polish team, who will play an important role in the novel, as Carlos later comes to suspect that she was the one who alerted the police that the two etarras might be in the hotel.

The underground spring known as La Banyera de Samsó was about twenty minutes' walk from the hotel and, at first sight, it looked like a pool where rain had collected in the midst of the bushes and the undergrowth. However, it was not the inoffensive place that its appearance and name might lead one to expect. As anyone who went near it soon discovered, its waters were anything but calm, the surface shaken by a continual trembling. That apparent contradiction in terms – the movement of water in an enclosed space – was partly explained when the visitor discovered that the bubbles came from below and that the pool was, in fact, a spring, and the puzzle was completely solved when the same visitor made his or her second discovery: the supposed pool was not in fact a closed circle, it was broken at one point, by a crevasse that swallowed the water, swallowing it down for ever, down into a cavern where it would never again see the light of the sun. There was a channel for those waters, it even had a name – La Riera Blanca – but no one who came to the pool could remember ever having seen it full. Anyway, very few visitors were tempted to go to the pool. Bathing there was forbidden and it was difficult to get to. The path that linked it to the road had long been overgrown and anyone wanting to go there would be forced to cross the hotel grounds.

Carlos was fond of the place and he used to bathe there rather than at the hotel swimming pool. Like the bakery and his bedroom in the flat, the pool seemed to him a silent, protected place, set apart from the world, and he used to visit it when, bored with the bakery and bored with his room, he nevertheless preferred to be alone, or when the way of life that had been his for the last five years suddenly seemed excessively monotonous and he fancied dicing with danger by swimming too close to the crevasse in the rocks. The pool helped him too when he needed to block out the Rat's accusing voice, because he had only to submerge his head and hear the rumble of the water in his ears for that inner voice to become almost inaudible.

The day after Poland's victory over Belgium, Carlos kept the promise he'd made to the dogs during the previous evening's walk and he went down to the pool as soon as he'd finished his morning's work in the bakery. He'd been swimming there for about a quarter of an hour when Belle and Greta started barking, announcing the approach of someone, probably someone walking along the path. Although most of his head was submerged in the water – he was floating on his back – and he couldn't hear the barking clearly, he knew that the dogs were not barking at Giuomar or some other known person. The barking was aggressive.

At first, he decided to ignore the warning and to remain floating in the water, but the barking from Belle and Greta grew louder, ever more hostile, and, in the end, he had to sit up and pay attention. He saw a woman waving to him from the bank, telling him to carry on with his swim. It was the Polish team's interpreter, Danuta Wyca, Pascal's 'grandmother'. She was wearing a white cotton dress and a broad-brimmed straw hat. When Carlos showed no sign of moving, she indicated the book she had in her hand: he needn't worry about her, she would sit and read on one of the rocks near the bank while he finished bathing.

'Guiomar and Pascal are on their way', she announced, barely raising her voice. She waved her book at the two dogs. Belle and Greta's curiosity was a threat to the impeccable white of her dress.

Guiomar and Pascal took longer than expected to join her and, in the end, after ten minutes had passed, Carlos decided to get out. He couldn't concentrate when there were witnesses. Lying in the pool with his legs and arms outstretched, feeling the drops of moisture in his nostrils, gazing up at the blue sky until his eyes hurt, all that constituted an important part of his bathing ceremony; but the ceremony could only be carried out in solitude, or in the friendly company of someone like Guiomar or María Teresa. (pp. 57–8)

Bernardo Atxaga, *The Lone Man*, trans. Margaret Jull Costa (London: Harvill, 1996).

Notes

[1] A. Martín, 'Pròleg. Novel·les en la penombra', in A. Piquer Vidal and À. Martín Escribà, *Catalana i criminal. La novel·la detectivesca del segle XX* (Palma de Mallorca: Documenta, 2006), p. 9.

[2] Atxaga's novel is the only one studied here which has been translated into English.

[3] B. Anderson, *Imagined Communities: Reflections on the Origin and Spread of Nationalism* (London: Verso, 1991), p. 7.

[4] A. Young, *Imagining Crime: Textual Outlaws and Criminal Conversations* (London: Sage, 1996), p. 9.

[5] Ibid., p. 10.

[6] S. McCracken, *Pulp: Reading Popular Fiction* (Manchester: Manchester University Press, 1998), p. 63.

[7] Young, *Imagining Crime*, pp. 83, 95.

[8] McCracken, *Pulp*, pp. 53–4.

[9] C. Perriam, et al. *A New History of Spanish Writing: 1939 to the 1990s* (Oxford: Oxford University Press, 2000), p. 5; F. Parcerisas, 'La traducción en Cataluña', *Antípodas*, 5 (1993), 32.

[10] J. Labanyi, 'Censorship or the fear of mass culture', in H. Graham and J. Labanyi (eds), *Spanish Cultural Studies: An Introduction. The Struggle for Modernity* (Oxford: Oxford University Press, 1995), p. 211.

[11] K. A. Woolard, *Double Talk: Bilingualism and the Politics of Ethnicity in Catalonia* (Stanford: Stanford University Press, 1989), p. 33.

[12] C. Mar-Molinero, 'The politics of language: Spain's minority languages', in Graham and Labanyi (eds), *Spanish Cultural Studies*, p. 339.

[13] C. Mar-Molinero, 'Galician', in B. Jordan (ed.), *Spanish Culture and Society: The Essential Glossary* (London: Arnold, 2002), p. 96.

[14] The actual degree of responsibility for these and other areas varies markedly depending upon the degree of autonomy negotiated with the central government.

[15] For a detailed analysis of the debates about 'Castilian' versus 'Spanish', see C. Mar-Molinero, *The Politics of Language in the Spanish-Speaking World* (London: Routledge, 2000), pp. 86–92.

16 Reproduced in J. Webber and M. Strubell i Trueta, *The Catalan Language: Progress Towards Normalisation* (Sheffield: The Anglo-Catalan Society, 1991), p. 56.
17 J-A. Fernàndez, 'Becoming normal: cultural production and cultural policy in Catalonia', in Graham and Labanyi (eds), *Spanish Cultural Studies*, p. 344; J. M. Lasagabaster, 'The promotion of cultural production in Basque', in Graham and Labanyi (eds), *Spanish Cultural Studies*, p. 351; C. Perriam et al., *A New History of Spanish Writing*, p. 209; X. de Toro Santos, 'Negotiating Galician cultural identity', in Graham and Labanyi (eds), *Spanish Cultural Studies*, p. 350.
18 A. Piquer Vidal and À. Martín Escribà, *Catalana i criminal. La novel·la detectivesca del segle XX* (Palma de Mallorca: Documenta, 2006), p. 16.
19 P. Hart, 'The mystery as midwife: an interview with Maria-Antònia Oliver', *The Armchair Detective* (summer 1992), 332; J-A. Fernàndez, 'Becoming normal', pp. 342–3.
20 The series did, however, contain two novels written originally in Catalan: Manuel de Pedrolo's *Joc brut* (Playing Dirty) and *Mossegar-se la cua* (Biting One's Own Tail). Both novels were extremely successful.
21 F. Parcerisas, 'La traducción en Cataluña', 34.
22 Fuster's other crime novels include *Tarda, sessió contínua, 3'45* (1976, 3.45 Afternoon Session), *La corona valenciana* (1982, The Valencian Crown), *Les cartes d'Hèrcules Poirot* (1983, The Letters of Hercules Poirot), *Per quan vingui un altre juny* (1987, When June Comes Around Again) and *Vida de gos i altres claus de vidre* (1989, A Dog's Life and Other Glass Keys).
23 Hart, 'The mystery as midwife', 332.
24 D. Porter, *The Pursuit of Crime: Art and Ideology in Detective Fiction* (New Haven: Yale University Press, 1981), p. 132.
25 Ibid., p. 133.
26 J. Fuster, *Sota el signe de Sagitari* (Barcelona: La Magrana, 1986), pp. 11, 34, 54, 62, 79.
27 Ibid., pp. 102, 139.
28 Ibid., p. 163.
29 Ibid., p. 159.
30 Ibid., pp. 86, 87.
31 For a discussion of themes and tendencies in the Galician crime novel see S. Gaspar Porras, 'Dez anos de narrativa negra galega (cen anos de cine)', *Anuario de estudios literarios galegos* (1995), 111–26.
32 C. G. Reigosa, *Crime en Compostela* (Vigo: Xerais, 2000), p. 9.
33 Ibid., p. 33.
34 A. D. Smith, *National Identity* (London: Penguin, 1991), p. 74.
35 Reigosa, *Crime en Compostela*, p. 36.
36 Ibid.
37 Ibid., pp. 26, 33.

[38] Ibid., pp. 75–6.
[39] X. de Toro Santos, 'Negotiating Galician cultural identity', p. 346.
[40] Reigosa, *Crime en Compostela*, p. 20.
[41] Toro Santos, 'Negotiating Galician cultural identity', pp. 348–50.
[42] Reigosa, *Crime en Compostela*, p. 32.
[43] Ibid., p. 25.
[44] J. Cillero Goiriastuena, 'Sabuesos insólitos: reflejos de la identidad en varias novelas policíacas escritas en euskara', *Antípodas*, 18 (2007), 246.
[45] J. Gabilondo, 'Before Babel: global media, ethnic hybridity, and enjoyment in Basque culture', *Revista internacional de estudios vascos*, 44, 1 (1999), 17.
[46] Cillero Goiriastuena, 'Sabuesos insólitos', 247–8.
[47] For an analysis of these three writers see ibid., 245–63.
[48] B. Atxaga, *El hombre solo* (Barcelona: Ediciones B, 2004), p. 9.
[49] According to José Ángel Ascunce, Atxaga uses the real murder of a retired infantry colonel by two *etarras* as the starting point for this novel. See J. Á. Ascunce, *Bernardo Atxaga. Los demonios personales de un escritor* (San Sebastián: Santurrán, 2000), p. 123 n. 67.
[50] Atxaga, *El hombre solo*, p. 10.
[51] Ibid., p. 96.
[52] Ibid., p. 69.
[53] Ibid., pp. 221, 50.
[54] Atxaga uses the Polish team and the Solidarity movement led by Lech Walesa to draw a parallel between the failure of socialism and nationalism to respond adequately to people's needs.

Bibliography

Anderson, Benedict, *Imagined Communities: Reflections on the Origin and Spread of Nationalism* (London: Verso, 1991).

Ascunce, J. Á., *Bernardo Atxaga. Los demonios personales de un escritor* (San Sebastián: Saturrarán, 2000).

Atxaga, B., *The Lone Man*, trans. Margaret Jull Costa (London: Harvill, 1996).

——, *El hombre solo* (Barcelona: Ediciones B, 2004).

Cillero Goiriastuena, J., 'Sabuesos insólitos: reflejos de la identidad envarias novelas policíacas escritas en euskara', *Antípodas*, 18 (2007), 245–63.

Fernàndez, J-A. 'Becoming normal: cultural production and cultural policy in Catalonia', in H. Graham and J. Labanyi (eds), *Spanish Cultural Studies: An Introduction. The Struggle for Modernity* (Oxford: Oxford University Press, 1995), pp. 342–6.

Fuster, J., *Sota el signe de Sagitari* (Barcelona: La Magrana, 1986).

Gabilondo, J., 'Before Babel: global media, ethnic hybridity, and enjoyment in Basque culture', *Revista internacional de estudios vascos*, 44, 1 (1999), 7–49.

Gaspar Porras, S., 'Dez anos de narrativa negra galega (cen anos de cine)', *Anuario de estudios literarios galegos* (1995), 111–26.
Graham, H. and J. Labanyi (eds), *Spanish Cultural Studies: An Introduction. The Struggle for Modernity* (Oxford: Oxford University Press, 1995)
Hart, P., 'The mystery as midwife: an interview with Maria-Antònia Oliver', *The Armchair Detective* (summer 1992), 330–4.
Labanyi, J., 'Censorship or the fear of mass culture', in Graham and Labanyi (eds), *Spanish Cultural Studies*, pp. 207–14.
Lasagabaster, J. M., 'The promotion of cultural production in Basque', in Graham and Labanyi (eds), *Spanish Cultural Studies*, pp. 351–5.
Mar-Molinero, C., 'The politics of language: Spain's minority languages', in Graham and Labanyi (eds), *Spanish Cultural Studies*, pp. 336–42.
——, *The Politics of Language in the Spanish-Speaking World* (London: Routledge, 2000).
——, 'Galician', in B. Jordan (ed.), *Spanish Culture and Society: The Essential Glossary* (London: Arnold, 2002), p. 96.
Martín, A. 'Pròleg. Novel·les en la penombra', in A. Piquer Vidal and À. Martín Escribà, *Catalana i criminal. La novel·la detectivesca del segle XX* (Palma de Mallorca: Documenta, 2006), pp. 9–10.
McCracken, S., *Pulp: Reading Popular Fiction* (Manchester: Manchester University Press, 1998).
Parcerisas, F., 'La traducción en Cataluña.' *Antípodas*, 5 (1993), 27–37.
Perriam, C., et al., *A New History of Spanish Writing: 1939 to the 1990s* (Oxford: Oxford University Press, 2000).
Piquer Vidal, A. and À. Martín Escribà, *Catalana i criminal. La novel·la detectivesca del segle XX* (Palma de Mallorca: Documenta, 2006).
Porter, D., *The Pursuit of Crime: Art and Ideology in Detective Fiction* (New Haven: Yale University Press, 1981).
Reigosa, C. G., *Crime en Compostela* (Vigo: Xerais, 2000).
Smith, A. D., *National Identity* (London: Penguin, 1991).
Toro Santos, X. de, 'Negotiating Galician cultural identity', in Graham and Labanyi (eds), *Spanish Cultural Studies*, pp. 346–51.
Webber, J. and M. Strubell i Trueta, *The Catalan Language: Progress Towards Normalisation* (Sheffield: The Anglo-Catalan Society, 1991).
Woolard, K. A., *Double Talk: Bilingualism and the Politics of Ethnicity in Catalonia* (Stanford: Stanford University Press, 1989).
Young, A., *Imagining Crime: Textual Outlaws and Criminal Conversations* (London: Sage, 1996).

5

Spanish Women's Crime Fiction, 1980s–2000s: Subverting the Conventions of Genre and Gender

NANCY VOSBURG

One of the most significant developments in the Spanish crime novel in the 1980s and 1990s was the emergence of women as both creators and protagonists of the genre. In Spanish literature in general, the transition to democracy following the almost forty years of authoritarian rule by Francisco Franco was marked by an increased participation and recognition of women writers, as well as a renewed interest in and 'recuperation' of female writers throughout Spanish history who had been excluded from or marginalized by the Spanish literary canon. The post-Franco Spanish Constitution, ratified in 1977, specifically declared equality between men and women, setting the stage for increased opportunities for women to participate in the public arena. Like their male counterparts, who 'began to utilize the detective form as a vehicle for the expression of issues of concern pertinent to the democratization process', women writers also turned to the genre to articulate, interrogate and critique the changing sociopolitical landscape.[1] Women writing in the detective genre was not an entirely new phenomenon in Spain, however. Indeed, one of the early initiators of the genre was a woman: doña Emilia Pardo Bazán, the renowned late nineteenth-/early twentieth-century novelist and short-story writer. In her short novel, *La gota de sangre* (1911, The Drop of Blood), Pardo Bazán introduced Spanish readers to the British-style genre then in vogue, à la Arthur Conan Doyle, through her amateur sleuth Selva. As several of her critics have noted, however, Pardo Bazán's novel was more innovative than imitative as she rejected the repetitive formula of the classic English police novel (see, for example, Vázquez de Parga, Colmeiro and Paredes Núñez). Perhaps the most striking difference is found in the character and methodologies of her amateur sleuth, Mr Selva, whose investigation of a murder is enlightened by intuition and imagination, rather than the cold logic and rationality of a Sherlock Holmes. Selva's conduct is likewise questionable, as he facilitates the accomplice's escape while manoeuvering the criminal to commit suicide.

Another woman precursor was the highly acclaimed Catalan novelist, short-story writer, poet and painter, Mercè Rodoreda, who published *Crim* (Crime) in 1936, a parody of the British cozy enigma-style detective fiction popularized by Agatha Christie and her contemporaries. Even during the civil war years (1936–9), as scholar Shelley Godsland has discovered, women were producing crime fiction: Josefina de la Torre, writing under the pseudonym Laura de Cominges, published *El enigma de los ojos grises* (The Mystery of the Grey Eyes) in 1938, while Mercedes Ballesteros Gaibrois, using the pen name Rocq Morris, published *City Hotel* and *París-Niza*, in 1938 and 1939 respectively.

Women crime writers were fairly prevalent in Spain in the 1950s, although many of them wrote under anglicized or masculine pseudonyms, and their novels were typically set in a foreign land.[2] This was a common strategy employed by many writers of the first decades of the dictatorship to avoid problems with the strict censorship of the Franco regime. Perhaps the most prolific woman crime novelist of this period was Isabel Calvo de Aguilar, whose works include *Doce sarcófagos de oro* (1951, Twelve Golden Sarcophagi), *El misterio del palacio chino* (1951, The Mystery of the Chinese Palace), *La isla de los siete pecados* (1952, The Island of the Seven Sins) and *La danzarina inmóvil* (1954, The Immobile Dancer).[3] Maria-Aurèlia Capmany, another well-established Catalan writer, also turned to the genre with her *El jaqué de la democràcia* (1972, The Morning Coat of Democracy).

Lourdes Ortiz

While some of these early women writers, especially Pardo Bazán, Rodoreda and Capmany, played with the conventions of this formulaic genre, none was bold enough to renegotiate the gender conventions, creating instead conventional male protagonists. The creation of women detectives was a product of the political changes within Spain beginning in 1975, the year of Franco's death, as well as the economic and social changes that accompanied the transition from dictatorship to democracy, such as the rise of feminism, the globalization of the economy, the cult of consumerism and the burgeoning of popular culture, changes that were affecting Spain as much as other Western nations in the postmodern period.

As many critics of the Anglo-American hard-boiled novel have noted (for example, Walton and Jones, Klein, Irons and Paretsky), changes in society, above all those dealing with gender and sex roles, made possible a new conception of the detective hero. Walton and Jones, for example, underscore the fact that the detective novel, like other formulaic fictions, reflects the cultural polemics and the theoretical problems of contemporary society. There is a reciprocal relationship between popular fiction and culture at large as, on the one hand, it affirms existing values and beliefs while, on the other hand, it helps readers to assimilate changes in traditional modes of perception. If in the conventional hard-boiled novel a woman was cast as an antagonist or an accessory (the well-known femme fatale or the passive supplicant) of the masculine hero, the new women protagonists challenged this image, altering in the process the genre and gender codes of the hard-boiled novel. As Glenwood Irons has asserted: 'The new woman detective speaks from fiction to the real world we inhabit ... We could even affirm the she "detects with a vengeance" in order to highlight the different power relations between the sexes that are being produced in contemporary society.'[4]

The first woman-authored female detective who appeared in post-Franco Spain was Bárbara Arenas, a professional detective created by Lourdes Ortiz in her 1979 novel *Picadura mortal* (Mortal Sting), at the urging of her publishing company, Sedmay Ediciones.[5] Sedmay was evidently eager to cash in on the commercial success enjoyed by translations of foreign crime novels in the immediate post-Franco period. Ortiz turned to the American hard-boiled novel as a model, inverting gender roles and behaviour to accommodate her female protagonist. As the author subsequently admitted, the novel was a hastily written work that was not well received by the critics.[6] Hart, for example, noted that the simple inversion of gender roles resulted in a character that embodied few of the positive qualities that we expect from a male detective hero, and that Ortiz's protagonist was neither convincing as a woman nor a model to be imitated.[7] But Madrid-based Ortiz does have the distinction of creating the first female detective, and the circumstances around the publication of her novel illuminate three dramatic changes in Spanish culture in the early post-Franco period: first, women's increased participation in Spanish literary production; secondly, a renewed emphasis on a well-developed plot in Spanish literature, after the drastic experimentalism of the last years of the dictatorship; and, thirdly, the commercial success of foreign popular literature, particularly American hard-boiled and English crime novels in translation that quickly became best-sellers in the Spanish market.

Maria-Antònia Oliver's Lònia Guiu

Meanwhile, in Catalonia, a group of young but already established writers was likewise turning an eye to the hard-boiled novel as a vehicle through which to come to terms with the changing socio-political landscape. One of the most important changes for the Catalonian writer was, of course, the acceptance of cultural plurality in the post-Francoist state and the recuperation of Catalan as an officially recognized language. The Ofèlia Dracs collective, the group's publishing pseudonym (already discussed in chapter 4 of this volume), was interested in reviving popular fiction in Catalan, a niche that during the many years of dictatorship was filled by cheap paperbacks in Castilian. Among this group was Maria-Antònia Oliver, an already established literary writer of Mallorcan origins. Oliver's contribution to the Ofèlia Dracs crime story collection, *Negra i consentida* (Hard-Boiled and Spoiled), was 'On ets, Mònica?' ('Where Are You, Monica?'), which introduced a determined young female private investigator with a fetish for lipstick: feminist Appol·lònia (Lònia) Guiu.[8] Lònia, a Barcelona-based Mallorcan feminist like her creator, debuted as a private investigator hired to find the missing wife (Monica) of a wealthy developer. Oliver's fictional character was so popular that the author proceeded to write a trilogy of novels over the next decade with Lònia as her main character, putting a new spin on the predominant gender and genre conventions of the Spanish *novela negra*.

Oliver's first novel featuring Lònia was *Estudi en lila* (1986, Study in Lilac), an obvious play on Arthur Conan Doyle's first Sherlock Holmes mystery, *A Study in Scarlet*. The colour lilac orients the reader not only to the woman-centred world in which Lònia operates, but also the crimes against women that predominate in her novel ('Haven't you ever noticed the graffiti done in lilac saying "Against rape, castration?"'[9]). Lònia is handed a missing-person case of a teenaged Mallorcan runaway, Sebastiana, while almost simultaneously she is hired by an antiques collector, Elena Guadí, who wants to know the identity of three men who supposedly gave her a bounced cheque for a valuable antique. Lònia's investigations of the two cases reveal a common denominator between Sebastiana and Elena: both have been victims of rape. In the course of tracking the three men, Lònia finds herself in the midst of a more convoluted plot concerning illegal international arms shipments. Recognizing her own limitations, and bruised and battered both emotionally and physically from the two investigations, she wisely 'sells' the arms shipments case to a more experienced fictional detective, Lluís Arquer (obviously a nod to Raymond Chandler's

Lew Archer, discussed in the previous chapter), the protagonist of the *Clau de vidre* radio series by Jaume Fuster (Oliver's late husband), in exchange for a plane ticket to Australia. Sebastiana has committed suicide, Gaudí has wreaked vengeance by castrating the three men who raped her, and Lònia realizes that her own ethical principles have been compromised to some extent in both situations.

In Oliver's second Lònia Guiu novel, *Antípodes* (1988, Antipodes), the heroine finds herself enmeshed in a case involving the enslavement, drugging and forced prostitution of a wealthy young Mallorcan woman whom she has met on the plane on her way to Australia. After many harrowing adventures, the investigation ultimately leads her back to Mallorca, where she learns that the underlying motive is to wrest the young heiress's land from her for a major development project. In order to get the evidence she needs to solve the case, Lònia infiltrates the prostitution ring, pretending to be one of the drugged young women. The third novel, *El sol que fa l'ànec* (1994, Blue Roses for a Dead . . . Lady?), also takes place in Oliver's native Mallorca. In this, Lònia, again in search of a missing young woman, is confronted with the most nefarious crime yet: the sexual abuse of children for profit.

Oliver's Lònia Guiu series is enriched by a subtext running throughout the three novels that is an obvious wink to P. D. James's 1972 novel, *An Unsuitable Job for a Woman*. Oliver inserts a strong feminist discourse into her novels through both theme and style, first, by centring her mysteries on crimes against women and children and, secondly, by creating a protagonist who vociferously defends her right to agency and autonomy. Lònia speaks and acts from a woman's perspective, and her investigations inevitably lead her to interrogate the broader socio-economic system, patriarchal and capitalist. In her Lònia Guiu short story, and again in *Antípodes*, Oliver establishes a direct relationship between rape of women and the commercial 'rape' of the landscape, critiquing the violent and destructive attitudes towards both women and nature that are reinforced, and protected, through the juncture of patriarchy and capitalism.[10]

Gender awareness pervades the Lònia Guiu novels in the protagonist's relationships with her gay partner Quim and her friends, lovers, clients and villains. We are aware of Lònia as both a woman and a feminist, in her vulnerability to romance, vanity and guilt, on the one hand, and in the positively attributed independent tough-girl stance she manifests in her investigations. Indeed, the English title of Oliver's third novel (which in Catalan is nonsensical), *Blue Roses for a Dead . . .*

Lady?, was chosen by the American translator Kathleen McNerney to underscore the interrogation of 'ladylike behaviour' that is central to the novels.[11] Lònia's struggle to prove her competence as a woman private investigator is constantly undermined by her mother's unwillingness to accept the circumstance, and by Quim's perceived paternalistic need to 'protect' her. Lònia is no superhero, but she does know a few martial arts moves, and 'talks back' to male imposition of force or power through wisecracks. While at first she appears to emulate the cynicism typical of the male hard-boiled hero, the reader comes to realize that this is nothing more than posturing, for Lònia does care and does suffer when her actions bring harm to other women. In her dealings with women from differing socio-economic classes, Lònia's sense of solidarity with female crime victims is one of her primary motivators. Moreover, once enmeshed in Oliver's quick-paced plots, it becomes evident that Lònia's cynicism has more to do with the suffocating strictures of traditional female socialization in Spain and the slow pace of change than with the individual women with whom she is dealing.

Oliver's Lònia Guiu crime novels, which have been translated into English as well as several other languages, portray a believable character who has both defects and virtues. More importantly, Oliver is the only woman writer to date who has created a series of novels featuring a female private eye, and she was the first to insert a feminist discourse into a commercially successful masculinist genre, turning both genre and gender on their heads. In *Estudi en lila*, for example, Lònia does not intervene by calling in the police when she learns of Gaudí's plan for personal vengeance, which results in her being an accomplice to further crimes. Her ethical decisions stem from her feminist sense of solidarity with other women, as well as from her scepticism of the official Spanish institutions of law and order, the 'right arms' of the Franco regime, which were slow to change in the aftermath of the dictatorship. While the conventional hard-boiled hero often acts outside the jurisdiction of the law, Oliver's heroine openly defies the rules in such a way that it forces the reader to examine the shortcomings and the prevalent misogynistic attitudes within the criminal justice system and the social system as a whole.

Alicia Giménez-Bartlett's Petra Delicado

Oliver's novels enjoyed great popularity among Catalan readers, but were little known outside Catalonia, even though they had been translated into Castilian. In the 1990s, there emerged another woman detective, this time a member of the official state police apparatus, Police Inspector Petra Delicado. A creation of Alicia Giménez-Bartlett, another Barcelona-based writer, the Petra Delicado series was immediately accessible to readers throughout Spain since the novels were written in Castilian. To date, Giménez-Bartlett has published eight novels in the series: *Ritos de muerte* (1996, Rites of Death), *Día de perros* (1997, Dog Day), *Mensajeros de la oscuridad* (1999, Messengers of Darkness), *Muertes de papel* (2000, Prime Time Suspects), *Serpientes en el paraíso* (2002, Serpents in Paradise), *Un barco cargado de arroz* (2004, A Ship Loaded With Rice), *Nido vacío* (2007, Empty Nest) and *El silencio de los claustros* (2009, The Silence of the Cloisters). In addition, a thirteen-episode television series was developed based on Giménez-Bartlett's novels, starring Ana Belén as the protagonist. While these novels have been translated into several languages, only three of the novels have been translated into English to date.

When the central figure of a police procedural is female, this sub-genre of the detective novel 'can represent both the possibility of women's integration into the mainstream of society in equal partnership with men and the disruption of perceived social harmony within law enforcement agencies themselves'.[12] I would argue as well that few writers in Spain until the 1990s would have cast their hero as a police inspector: for many who grew up during the Franco period, the police were the instrument of an oppressive regime. Police, particularly corrupt police, as well as wealthy industrialists, were more likely to be portrayed, if not as criminals, then at least as accomplices to the crimes, untrustworthy and brutal (see Hart's discussion of the Lorenzo Silva novels in chapter 2, for example). The appearance of a fictional female police inspector thus speaks to two important changes in Spain that were finally becoming 'normalized' some twenty years after the death of the dictator. On the one hand, perceptions about the trustworthiness of a police force as a democratic institution whose purpose is citizen protection rather than citizen harassment had clearly begun to be inculcated in society. On the other, under the democratic constitution guaranteeing the equality of men and women, the latter were making dramatic headway into professions previously dominated by men. In Giménez-Bartlett's Petra Delicado series, however, neither of these situations is rendered as completely 'normalized': until her first case in *Ritos de muerte*, Petra has been assigned to the documents department of the force, and during the course of her investigations, the reader sees on many occasions a citizenry reluctant to cooperate with the police, who are still viewed with cautious scepticism throughout the country.

The crimes committed in this first Petra novel are a series of rapes. Like Oliver, Giménez-Bartlett chose crimes against women as her first foray into the genre. Perhaps it is the nature of rape, which objectifies, depersonalizes and victimizes women, which provides a stark counterpoint for a fictional woman detective to demonstrate her subjective agency in righting the wrong. Petra, a former lawyer and twice divorced, has little sense of female solidarity, however, and prefers to be treated as 'un compañero más' (just another [male] colleague).[13] While Petra looks on the young women in her gym as potential rape victims, she does not acknowledge that she, too, could be one, nor is her sexual intimacy ever threatened. Thus, Petra stands in stark contrast to Oliver's Lònia, who on several occasions is threatened by rape or sexual assault.

As some critics of Giménez-Bartlett's novels have observed, Petra's lack of empathy, or even sympathy, for the victims is emblematic of a 'post-feminist' construction of the character (see Godsland and Molinaro, for example). In Giménez-Bartlett's subsequent novels, the themes focus on individual deviancy or on crimes committed by small groups of individuals whose motives are personal gain. While Lònia also battles criminals with similar motives, the emphasis in Oliver's novels is always on the myriad ways in which the deviant behaviour of men affects women. Petra, on the contrary, shares the same 'tough' attitudes of her male colleagues, not only towards the victims of sexual crimes, but particularly towards marginalized sectors of society such as the unskilled working class and the homeless.

If, from a feminist perspective, Petra Delicado is constructed within a 'post-feminist' context which coincides with her late 1990s historical period, this is not to say that the series does not address women's continuing negotiation of sexism within government institutions and the society as a whole. Giménez-Bartlett has endowed her character with a subaltern, Fermín Garzón, who, much in the vein of Quijote's Sancho, becomes a site for mediating different perceptions of reality, in this case the changing attitudes and values concerning women versus traditional ways of seeing. The relationship between Petra and Garzón enriches the reader's understanding of Petra's motives and behaviour, while reminding us that much has yet to be achieved for women intent on breaking through the glass ceiling. Even the name that the author chose for her protagonist suggests the internal conflicts that women confront in the post-feminist age: while she can be hard as a rock (Petra/*piedra*) in carrying out her professional duties, especially when confronting possible suspects or villains, she often yearns for the tranquillity of a normal domestic life (Delicado/delicate).

Giménez-Bartlett's texts are especially valuable in the way in which they fictionally 'document' sociological trends in post-Franco Spain, from the evolving attitudes about the female victims of sexual assault (*Ritos de muerte*), to the commercial apparatus that has grown up around pets (*Día de perros)*, to the rise in quasi-religious sects engaged in brainwashing young adolescents (*Mensajeros de la oscuridad*), to the money-laundering of Russian mafiosos in Barcelona (*Mensajeros de la oscuridad*), to the fleeing of the upper middle-class from the city to the suburbs as downtown properties become unaffordable (*Serpientes en el paraíso),* to the exploitation of immigrant women and children (as nannies and housecleaners to well-to-do families in *Serpientes* and as mafia-controlled prostitutes and thieves in *Nido vacío*), to the increasing numbers and the plight of the homeless (*Un barco cargado de arroz*) and to dysfunctional families (*Nido vacío*), to name just a few. Giménez-Bartlett places emphasis on class issues, primarily to highlight the fact that the crimes and misdemeanours committed in her novels are not limited to a specific class (just as they are not limited to a specific gender). As Petra discovers, 'los palacios y las chabolas están conectadas por alcantarillas' (the palaces and the shacks are connected by the sewers).[14]

Giménez-Bartlett has enjoyed much more commercial success with her Petra Delicado series than has Oliver, perhaps because she has created a character that is essentially more 'mainstream': middle class, educated, heterosexual, Castilian speaking and not a feminist. As both Oliver and Giménez-Bartlett have demonstrated, however, crime fiction has become a convenient vehicle for examining issues pertinent to women in an ever changing society. And one of those issues, that of lesbian visibility and equal rights for gays and lesbians, leads us to a third author who has created a detective series, the Barcelona-based Isabel Franc.

Isabel Franc's lesbian soap operas

It is worth noting that one of the predominant trends in recent Spanish lesbian literature has been the use of the formulaic conventions of crime fiction, a trend that was also seen in the United States during the 1970s and 1980s. Barbara Sjoholm (the former Barbara Wilson), one of the initiators of the genre in the US, has spoken of the possibilities that the lesbian thriller, such as her Pam Nilsson mysteries, offers in terms of contesting the ideologies that have forced lesbians to play the role of the silent victims of crimes against women.[15] For Sjoholm, the fact that a lesbian becomes the investigator, instead of the victim, offers opportunities to bring about a justice many times denied to lesbians. It comes as no surprise that differences in sexual orientation would come into play in women's rewriting of the genre, which offers a controlled space that enables a wide audience to contest established categories, conventions and stereotypes. Isabel Franc, writing under the pseudonym Lola Van Guardia, began publishing in the late 1990s a trilogy of 'culebrones lésbicos' (lesbian soap operas) adhering to a lesbian-utopian aesthetic of only admitting female characters, as well as using the feminine as the generic universal. The second and third instalments of the series, *Plumas de doble filo* (2000, Double-Edged Feathers/Pens) and *La mansión de las tríbadas* (2002, The Mansion of the Tribades), are parodies of the detective novel that deliciously demythify the male hard-boiled hero. The female detective, Emma García, a fan of *The X-File*'s Agent Scully, is a hard-nosed Madrid police inspector by day, lesbian aspiring femme fatale by night, whose passion for women (particularly the prime suspects) often interferes with the hard work, persistence and logical approach required to solve the crime. García is burdened by additional obstacles: her regulation uniform skirt prevents her from being the action hero who nabs the suspect at a decisive moment in *Plumas*, and her allergies to liquour and smoke likewise interfere with her hard-boiled self-image and her ability to remain inconspicuous as she stakes out possible suspects in Barcelona's night spots. According to the author, García was originally created to poke fun at the often acrimonious imposition of the Spanish central government on the autonomous Catalan periphery but, despite her tough exterior and crude language, the bumbling, sentimental character became an endearing figure to both the author and her readers. And since she is rendered as a parody, the novels serve to highlight precisely those conventions that we often find in the hard-boiled masculine heroes of this formulaic genre.

In *Plumas de doble filo*, García is sent to Barcelona after the dead body, presumably that of the Barcelona-based Member of Parliament Laura Mayo, is found in her garden, her face and hands scorched beyond recognition on her barbecue. While in Barcelona, Inspector García is aided not only by the women of the Catalan autonomous police force (*les Mosses d'Esquadra*), particularly Agent Montse Murals, but by an entire lesbian community that collectively contributes to the resolution of the crime. In *La mansión de las tríbadas*, García finds herself once again in Catalonia, on holiday at a newly opened lesbian bed-and-breakfast hotel in the country while on a forced break from her job. García, preoccupied with a lump in her breast, soon finds herself caught up in a mysterious disappearance and arson at the bed and breakfast. She is once again aided by the assembled cast of lesbians that figure throughout the trilogy.

Franc, collaborating with her fictitious alter ego Lola Van Guardia, subsequently wrote an additional novel featuring Inspector García, *No me llames cariño* (2004, Don't Call Me Darling). Unlike the trilogy, this novel about an avenging angel of domestic abuse victims features male characters as well, as Franc/Van Guardia responds to the upsurge in domestic violence throughout Spain. Inspector García has officially transferred to the Catalan autonomous police force (and, therefore, must learn Catalan, as is required of all autonomous government employees), but the case she must solve pits her against a feminist community that is fed up with the lack of adequate legislation and police measures to counter domestic abuse. As the dead bodies of alleged domestic abusers begin to pile up, each with a pink ribbon tied around his penis, García surrounds herself with a team of professional women: psychologist Carol Choy, forensic doctor Marisa Giménez, lawyer Helena Mayoral and, of course, Agent Montse Murals. Little does she know that the assassin is one of the members of her team.

While Isabel Franc/Lola Van Guardia employs the crime novel format as a plotting device in her humorous novels, her main objective is to capture the differing attitudes towards lesbian sexuality from both within and outside the community and to make 'visible' the presence of lesbians throughout society. More importantly, we see lesbians' battles against discrimination by the conservative political, judicial and social system of the late 1990s and early 2000s, all delivered in a humorous yet melodramatic style typical of an engaging *culebrón* (soap opera). Other Spanish lesbian writers who have used the crime novel format as a plotting device are Lais Arcos in her *72 horas* (2004, 72 Hours) and Marta Fagés with *Amores prohibidos* (2004, Forbidden Loves). Blanca Alvarez, in her 1991 *La soledad del monstruo* (The Loneliness of the Monster) and its sequel, *Las niñas no hacen ruido cuando mueren* (1998, Girls Don't Make Noise When They Die), has also created a lesbian character, Bárbara Villalta, an anti-heroine in the true sense of the word, detested and derided by all. Hers is a universe of unremitting violence against women of all ages and social classes, in which even 'Bab' commits brutal acts against other women.[16]

Mercedes Castro's Clara Deza

It is perhaps not surprising, given the perennial problem of the glass ceiling in westernized societies and the enduring presence of Spanish machismo, particularly in previously male-dominated professions, that the suitability and ability of women to exercise autonomy and agency as private investigators or members of an institutional police force continues to provide a subtext in more recent women-authored crime fiction. Such is the case with *Y punto* (2008, Enough Said), a lengthy first novel by Mercedes Castro. Madrid police detective Clara Deza, the protagonist of the novel, is another woman caught between two competing universes: the professional one, in which she is surrounded by male colleagues who either deride her or overprotect her, and the personal one, as the wife of a lawyer who also often fails to understand her. In many ways, Clara Deza is a much tougher, more cynical version of Giménez-Bartlett's Petra Delicado. Castro portrays her as a woman caught up in the post-feminist dilemma: she takes for granted her right to agency and autonomy, yet still has to battle the not-so-visible sexism that not only undermines a woman's professional advancement but continues to burden her with the larger share of domestic responsibility.

Rosa Ribas – Between Two Waters

Nonetheless, there are other themes emerging in the genre that mirror both developments in Spanish crime fiction in general and the current socio-political concerns that the nation is facing. One of the most interesting recent novels, billed as 'un caso de la comisaria Cornelia Weber-Tejedor' (a case of Commissioner Cornelia Weber-Tejedor), is Rosa Ribas's 2007 *Entre dos aguas* (Between Two Waters), winner of the Brigada 21 Prize for best first *novela negra*. The action of the novel takes place in Frankfurt, Germany, and focuses primarily on the Spanish community there that emigrated from their homeland in the aftermath of Spain's civil war. Cornelia, the daughter of a German father and a Spanish mother (like her creator, Ribas), is assigned to investigate the death of Marcelino Soto, a successful restaurant owner who was involved in the exile community's activities.

Cornelia's investigation of Soto's death leads her into a confrontation with her own family's past as she discovers old grudges stemming from the Spanish Civil War and the ensuing mass exodus of Republican sympathizers from the homeland that, despite the distance in time and space, provide clues to the current events. She herself is caught 'between two waters', not only because she represents the authority of the German government, viewed suspiciously by the Spanish exile community that is reluctant to air its 'dirty linen' in the host country, but also because of the ongoing strain of gender relations, which, despite legislation to the contrary, continue to be a source of unnecessary conflict in the workforce. Interestingly enough, the publication of Ribas's novel coincided with the debates in the Spanish legislature on the Law of Historical Memory (approved in October 2007), which sought to recuperate a past that had all but been obliterated, first by the Franco regime, and subsequently by the new democratic society that, euphoric and yet fragile, was determined to forget the conflicts leading up to the Spanish Civil War and its aftermath in order to forge the future. As Ribas's novel reflects, this past, which to all appearances has been buried, continues to haunt the national psyche, both abroad and in the homeland.

Ribas has published two additional Cornelia Weber-Tejado novels, *Con anuncio* (2009, Forewarned), a case dealing with the Frankfurt financial world, and *En caída libre* (2011, Freefall), which centers on drug-trafficking through the Frankfurt airport.

Conclusion

Spanish women writers are also contributing their voice and gendered perceptions to another sub-genre of crime fiction that has gained tremendous popularity in recent years, the espionage novel or political thriller. Writers such as the Catalans Anna Grau, with her novel *El dia que va morir el president* (1999, The Day the President Died), and Assumpta Maresma, author of *El complot dels anells* (1988, The Conspiracy of the Rings), have employed this genre to explore the relationships between gender and national identity, a question that, as we have seen in chapter 4, looms large in writings from the major autonomous communities. Having been denied participation in state institutions and in the nation-building endeavour prior to the advent of democracy, women were generally absent from the male action and masculine world-view that typically characterized spy thrillers. Both Grau and Maresma position their female characters as leaders in the struggle for Catalan nationalism, political activists who are involved in the decision-making process of nation building.

There are several other Spanish women writers who have ventured as well with women protagonists into the various sub-genres of crime fiction, although, with the exception of Maria-Antònia Oliver, Alicia Giménez-Bartlett, Rosa Ribas and Isabel Franc, none has created a series detective. Among those who have experimented with women-driven crime fiction are Margarita Aritzeta, whose *El cau del llop* (1992, The Wolf's Lair) features female detective Coia Moreno, Isabel-Clara Simó, who published *Una sombra fosca com un núvol de tempesta* (translated as A Corpse of One's Own) in 1991, featuring amateur sleuth Sara Costa, Asumpta Margenat, whose *Escapa't d'Andorra* (1989, translated as Wild Card) centers on a female thief, and Matilde Asensi, who also presents us with a successful female thief in *El salon de ámbar* (1999, The Amber Room). Revision of the hard-boiled tradition in Spain by women authors employing women detectives offers a subversive potential for critiquing the cultural norms not only underlying the original American hard-boiled literary tradition but integrated into the crime genre by practitioners in Spain. These women-driven novels bring to the forefront the changing landscape around issues of sex, gender and national identity in democratic Spain, while at the same time allowing the authors to enjoy the burgeoning commercial success of the genre.

* * *

Extract from *Estudi en Lila* (Study in Lilac) by Maria-Antònia Oliver

She [Elena Gaudí] didn't give me a chance to say that those subterfuges weren't necessary. Nor that I usually didn't accept my clients telling me how to do my job. But the truth is that I liked the gal so I hadn't said anything like that even though she was there for quite a while. It was fine that she hadn't told me her sordid story as if I were on the other side of a confessional or a social worker. I could leave that up to Jerònia, whose vocation was helping others, and I would do my own job.

I heard the toilet flushing – more noisily than usual, as if Quim had really yanked it.

Just as Mrs Elena Gaudí closed the office door with the same gentleness with which she had opened it, he came out, annoyed and sweaty. The odor from the bathroom cut through the cloud of the perfume the new client had left behind.

'What did that amazon want?' With one hand he wiped his sweaty brow and with the other zipped up his pants.

'Don't tell me you didn't hear every word. And she's not an amazon. You men wear blinders, pal. If women don't spell everything out, men never seem to catch on. And would you do me the damn favor of zipping up your pants inside the bathroom? Even in that way you men show off your sense of power.'

'Hey, hold that steam-roller tongue of yours. If you're mad at the lady, get mad at her, okay?'

'I'm not mad at anyone. It's just that sometimes male indiscretion gets to me.'

'Now you're talking like Mercè. But I'm glad you recognize me as a male. I've been plenty discreet already today. Don't you think it's asking a lot to be on the throne all that time?'

I imagined him sitting on the toilet, trying to listen to the conversation, and I burst into genuine laughter.

'And now you're laughing, crazy lady.'

'Did you hear her, or not?'

'Of course!'

'She really made up a story! But it reeks of a love story and nothing else.'

'Ha! She's too skinny to have love stories like that! That she didn't tell you the truth is clear as a bell, but don't make up romances, Paloni.'

'Don't call me Paloni, dammit!'

'Paloni is much more exotic than Lònia, dear! And don't tell me to call you Apol·lònia. You sound like a Roman empress if you don't shorten your name.'

'I just don't like the sound of it, and that's all. It's a romance, I'm telling you. But did you get a good look at that lady?'

'No way. I like the flashy ones, myself.'

'You don't have your eyes in the back of your head, pal. You've got them on the end of your . . .'

'Discretion, sweetie, discretion!'

And we started to map out the job. Quim bawled me out for not having insisted on more information about the check, and for not having asked for a description of the three men.

'If I already know it's a story . . . why press the point?'

'That's the very reason, see?'

He was surprised when I put him in charge of the lost girl and I took on the job of the antique dealer.

'Just find out if the card she left me is genuine, and not another trick, and that's all you have to do. I'll do all the rest.'

'I can't understand it! What would Jerònia think if she knew you left the case she recommended in the hands of a servant?'

In the end, Quim was as curious as I was about Mrs--or Miss? Gaudí. He was clearly playing it cool; he wasn't as blind as he wanted me to think. But it was me who had the license, the office, and who paid the yearly fees; I called him a partner because I wanted to, but in reality he was hired help. So I was the one who chose which job to do, and distributed the others. I was more interested in the antique dealer than in the girl. I wanted to know why she had lied to me.

Maria-Antònia Oliver, *Study in Lilac*, trans. Kathleen McNerney (Seattle: Seal Press, 1987), pp. 9–11.

Notes

1. Renée W. Craig-Odders, '*Realismo crítico* and the narrative strategy in post-Franco Spanish detective fiction: the case of Andreu Martín', *Romance Languages Annual*, 8 (1997), 417.
2. Shelley Godsland, *Killing Carmens: Women's Crime Fiction from Spain* (Cardiff: University of Wales Press, 2007), p. 3.
3. Ibid.
4. Glenwood Irons (ed.), *Feminism in Women's Detective Fiction* (Toronto: University of Toronto Press, 1995), p. xv.
5. Patricia Hart, *The Spanish Sleuth: The Detective in Spanish Fiction* (Cranbury, NJ and London: Associated University Presses, 1987), p.172.
6. Ibid.
7. Ibid., p.173.
8. The English translation of Oliver's short story, 'Where Are You, Monica?' was subsequently published in an anthology of international crime stories, *A Woman's Eye* (New York: Delacorte Press, 1991), edited by the American queen of the genre, Sara Paretsky.
9. Maria-Antònia Oliver, *Study in Lilac*, trans. Kathleen McNerney (Seattle: Seal Press, 1987), p.155.
10. Two of Oliver's earlier novels, *Croniques d'un mig estiu* (1970) and *Cronique de la molt anomenada ciutat de Montcarrà* (1972) were also concerned with unbridled development on her native island of Mallorca.
11. The title was suggested to McNerney by Patricia Hart, author of *The Spanish Sleuth*, who wrote the preface to the English translation.
12. Priscilla L. Walton and Manina Jones, *Detective Agency: Women Rewriting the Hard-Boiled Tradition* (Berkeley: University of California Press, 1999), p. 14.
13. Alicia Giménez-Bartlett, *Ritos de muerte* [Rites of Death] (Barcelona: Grijalbo, 1996), p. 58.
14. Allicia Giménez-Bartlett, *Día de perros* [Dog Day] (Barcelona: Grijalbo, 1997), p. 112.
15. Barbara Wilson, 'The outside edge: lesbian mysteries', *Para-doxa: Studies in World Literary Genres*, 1 (1995), 176–86.
16. Godsland, *Killing Carmens*, p. 97.

Bibliography

Alvarez, Blanca, *La soledad del monstruo* [The Loneliness of the Monster] (Madrid: Grupo Libro 88, 1991).

—, *Las niñas no hacen ruido cuando mueren* [Girls Don't Make Noise When They Die] (Premià del Mar: El Clavell, 1998).

Arcos, Lais, *72 horas* [72 Hours] (Barcelona: La Tempestad, 2004).

Aritzeta, Margarita, *El clau del llop* [The Wolf's Lair] (Barcelona: Magrana, 1992).

Asensi, Matilde, *El salón de ámbar* [The Amber Room] (Barcelona: Plaza y Janes, 1999).

Castro, Mercedes, *Y punto* [Enough Said] (Madrid: Alfaguara, 2008).

Colmeiro, José F., 'Relectura de la novela policiaca: *La gota de sangre* de E. Pardo Bazán', *Hispanic Journal*, 10, 2 (spring 1989), 33–48.

Craig-Odders, Renée W., '*Realismo critic* and the narrative strategy in post-Franco Spanish detective fiction: the case of Andreu Martín', *Romance Languages Annual*, 8 (1997), 417.

Giménez-Bartlett, Alicia, *Ritos de muerte* [Rites of Death] (Barcelona: Grijalbo, 1996).

——, *Día de perros* [Dog Day] (Barcelona: Grijalbo, 1997).

——, *Mensajeros de la oscuridad* [Messengers of Darkness] (Barcelona: Plaza y Janés, 1999).

——, *Muertes de papel* [Prime Time Suspects] (Barcelona: Plaza y Janés, 2000).

——, *Serpientes en el paraíso* [Serpents in Paradise] (Barcelona: Planeta, 2002).

——, *Un barco cargado de arroz* [A Ship Loaded With Rice] (Barcelona: Planeta, 2004).

——, *Nido vacío* [Empty Nest] (Barcelona: Planeta, 2006).

——, *El silencio de los claustros* [The Silence of the Cloisters] (Barcelona: Destino, 2009).

Godsland, Shelley, 'From feminism to postfeminism in women's detective fiction from Spain: the case of Maria-Antònia Oliver and Alicia Giménez-Bartlett', *Letras femeninas*, 28, 1 (summer 2002), 84–99.

——, *Killing Carmens: Women's Crime Fiction from Spain* (Cardiff: University of Wales Press, 2007).

Grau, Anna, *El dia que va morir el president* [The Day the President Died] (Barcelona: Empúries, 1999).

Hart, Patricia, *The Spanish Sleuth: The Detective in Spanish Fiction* (Cranbury, NJ and London: Associated University Presses, 1987).

Irons, Glenwood (ed.) *Feminism in Women's Detective Fiction* (Toronto: University of Toronto Press, 1995).

Klein, Kathleen Gregory, '*Habeas Corpus*: feminism and detective fiction', in Irons (ed.), *Feminism in Women's Detective Fiction* (Toronto: University of Toronto Press, 1995), pp. 175–85.

Maresma, Assumpta, *El complot dels anells* [The Conspiracy of the Rings] (Barcelona: Magrana, 1988).
Margenat, Assumpta, *Escapa't d'Andorra* [Wild Card] (Barcelona: Magrana, 1989).
Molinaro, Nina L., 'Writing the wrong rites? Rape and women's detective fiction in Spain', *Letras femeninas*, 28, 1 (summer 2002), 100–17.
Oliver, Maria-Antònia, *Estudi en lila* [*Study in Lilac*] (Barcelona: Magrana, 1985).
——, *Study in Lilac*, trans. Kathleen McNerney (Seattle: Seal Press, 1987).
——, *Antípodes* (Barcelona: Magrana, 1988).
——, *Antipodes*, trans. Kathleen McNerney (Seattle: Seal Press, 1989).
——, *El sol que fa l'ànec* (Barcelona: Magrana, 1994).
——, *Blue Roses for a Dead . . . Lady?*, trans. Kathleen McNerney (Sewanee, TN: University of the South Press, 1998).
Paredes Núñez, Juan (ed.), *La novela policiaca española* (Granada: Universidad de Granada, 1989), p. 10.
Paretsky, Sara (ed.), *A Woman's Eye* (New York: Delacorte Press, 1991).
Ribas, Rosa, *Entre dos aguas* [Between Two Waters] (Barcelona: Ediciones Urano, 2007).
——, *Con anuncio* [Forewarned] (Barcelona: Viceversa, 2009).
——, *En caída libre* [Free fall] (Barcelona: Viceversa, 2011).
Simó, Isabel-Clara, *Una ombra fosca com un núvol de tempesta* [A Corpse of One's Own] (Barcelona: Area, 1991).
Van Guardia, Lola, *Plumas de doble filo* [Double-Edged Feathers/Pens] (Barcelona: EGALES, 1999).
——, *La mansión de las tríbadas* [The Mansion of the Tribades] (Barcelona: EGALES, 2002).
——, *No me llames cariño* [Don't Call Me Darling] (Barcelona: EGALES, 2004).
Vázquez de Parga, Salvador, *La novela policiaca en España* (Barcelona: Ronsel, 1993).
Vosburg, Nancy, 'Genre bending: Maria-Antònia Oliver's Catalan sleuth', *Letras femeninas*, 28, 1 (summer 2002), 57–70.
Walton, Priscilla L. and Manina Jones, *Detective Agency: Women Rewriting the Hard-Boiled Tradition* (Berkeley: University of California Press, 1999).
Wilson, Barbara, 'The outside ledge: lesbian mysteries', *Para-doxa: Studies in World Literary Genres*, 1 (1995), 176–86.

6
Spanish Crime Fiction: 2001 and Beyond

DAVID KNUTSON

The last quarter of the twentieth century was a period of intense production in the history of crime fiction in Spain, although the trend slowed in the 1990s. Pioneering writers aged, and few rising stars were making themselves known. The start of the twenty-first century could have been the end of an era. Manuel Vázquez Montalbán, a hugely significant author, passed away, and there were no assurances that others would take his place. However, the first decade of this millennium has demonstrated that crime fiction has achieved a general penetration into contemporary Spanish cultural production. The genre has expanded beyond initial conceptions, growing to encompass a variety of themes that blend into other important types of popular fiction. This decade has shown that crime fiction no longer depends on a limited number of key authors, and that the form now takes different directions as younger authors appropriate the conventions to apply them in new context.

The end of Manuel Vázquez Montalbán's career

The year 2003 truly was a milestone, and some observers probably feared that it would be the end of crime fiction in Spain. The sudden death of writer Manuel Vázquez Montalbán, who collapsed in Bangkok airport on 18 October during a tour of Asia and the Pacific, prematurely ended the career of the author considered by most to be the foremost Spanish crime writer in history (see chapter 3 in this volume). Vázquez Montalbán was certainly not the only participant in the explosion of the publication of crime novels that accompanied the Spanish transition to democracy of the 1970s and 1980s, but there is no debate about his leading role in the trend. Scholarship on other novelists is widely available, but Manuel Vázquez Montalbán is still by and large the starting point in the study of recent Spanish detective writing. Even a writer of the stature of Eduardo Mendoza believes that Vázquez Montalbán has been 'el punto de referencia de nuestro tiempo' (the reference point of our time).[1]

Private investigator Pepe Carvalho began his prolific series of cases with *Yo maté a Kennedy* (1972, I Killed Kennedy) and *Tatuaje* (1974, Tattoo), the first two novels in what came to be known as the *Serie Carvalho* (Carvalho Series). He was a regular (though not exclusive) fixture in Vázquez Montalbán's fiction through the posthumous release of the two volumes of *Milenio Carvalho – Rumbo a Kabul* and *En las Antípodas* (Millennium Carvalho – On the Road to Kabul and In the Antipodes), early in 2004. The series developed into a vehicle for the author to express his disappointment with the outcomes of Spain's transition from the dictatorship of Francisco Franco (which ended in 1975) to democracy. As Mari Paz Balibrea makes evident in chapter 3, the dream of a utopian society that anti-Francoists such as Vázquez Montalbán had kept alive for years was dashed when elected governments opted for market-driven policies that turned Spain into another consumer society in a capitalistic world. Caragh Wells confirms the author's disappointment over Spain's turning away from its recent past: 'Vázquez Montalbán expressed . . . concern at Spanish society's apparent willingness to ignore or forget the memory of those who had fought against Franco and then struggled to survive under his dictatorship.'[2]

Vázquez Montalbán's disillusionment intensified as his home city of Barcelona undertook urban renewal programmes in the 1980s and 1990s. At the end of the twentieth century, the city had been transformed to the extent that Carvalho no longer recognizes it, and the detective sets out to investigate cases in other parts of the world. According to José V. Saval, *Milenio I* and *II* (Millennium I and II), the only Carvalho novel(s) published in the first decade of the twenty-first century, were conceived as a farewell for the detective.[3] In the first volume, *Rumbo a Kabul*, Carvalho murders an antagonist and flees Barcelona with his assistant Biscuter. The pair trek through Israel, Turkey, India and Greece, ending up in Afghanistan. The second volume, *En las Antípodas*, continues the itinerary towards the South Pacific, where Carvalho returns to locations, such as Thailand and Argentina, visited in previous novels. Carvalho is arrested on his return to Barcelona, and the series necessarily ends there. Saval believes that Vázquez Montalbán would have found a way to continue Carvalho's life in some way or another, but the author's unexpected death effectively closes the book on the lives of both character and author.[4]

Ironically, Vázquez Montalbán's passing may be a point at which a wider view of Spanish crime fiction becomes possible. He earned a great deal of attention in the public and the academic world, and it is no overstatement to declare his pre-eminance in criticism and scholarship on Spanish crime fiction. The laudatory remembrances of his life indicate genuine sorrow over his passing and, several years later, prominent figures still mourn the loss of his friendship, example and inspiration. All admiration aside, the disappearance of the key figure has required publishers, critics and readers to direct their interests towards other authors, some of whom are veterans who have enhanced their literary profiles in this decade as well as others who are beginning their own rise to prominence.

Francisco González Ledesma

One example of the former is Francisco González Ledesma (1927–), a Barcelona writer with a life similar to Vázquez Montalbán's, except for his relative obscurity. González Ledesma observes that Francoist censors prevented him from publishing under his own name for many years.[5] During that time, he wrote cheap kiosk novels under various pseudonyms (such as Silver Kane) in the 1950s and 1960s. During the transition to democracy, he participated in the *novela negra* boom with several novels in the 1980s, but he never achieved the fame and fortune of Manuel Vázquez Montalbán, despite having much in common with the late author. Inspector Méndez, González Ledesma's detective character, appears in novels such as *Crónica sentimental en rojo* (Sentimental Chronicle in Red), the Planeta prize winner in 1984, and *La dama de Cachemira* (1986, The Cashmere Lady). Although Méndez is a police officer, he shares much with private detective Pepe Carvalho, just as González Ledesma and Vázquez Montalbán are from similar backgrounds. Both authors and characters grew up in working-class families in modest neighbourhoods of Barcelona, and each has expressed a high degree of dissatisfaction with the results of Spain's democratic transition. Just as Vázquez Montalbán criticizes urban development in Barcelona, González Ledesma laments what has happened to the city.[6] However, González Ledesma did not subsequently create a consistent *Serie Méndez* (Méndez Series) in the manner of the Carvalho series, and González Ledesma seems to suggest that political interests lie behind his low production during the 1980s: 'También es cierto que me han tumbado novelas, incluso tras ganar el Planeta' (It is also true that they have buried some of my novels, even after I won the Planeta prize).[7] Unfortunately, he provides no further details to explain the gap.

Méndez did not reappear consistently until the first decade of the twenty-first century, but then quickly recovered from these years of neglect. González Ledesma's earlier novels (even the pulp fiction of Silver Kane) have been re-edited. He won the 2002 Hammett Prize with *El pecado o algo parecido* (Sin, or Something Like It) and *Una novela de barrio* (A Neighbourhood Novel) earned him the first Premio Internacional de Novela Negra RBA (The International RBA *Novela Negra* Prize) in 2007. Between these two publications, González Ledesma was also awarded the first Premio Carvalho (Carvalho Prize) in 2005. These later novels continue the ageless Méndez's attempts to repair injustices that are beyond – and even caused by – the legal system. Rosa Mora describes the officer's career:

> De joven, Méndez, mil veces entrenado en los sótanos de Via Laietana, fue policía de la Brigada Criminal franquista, pero llevaba bocadillos a los rojos detenidos y les servía de correo. Ahora, el viejo poli trabaja en la comisaría de Nou de la Rambla, alguna vez le han confinado a los archivos y sabe que nunca ascenderá ni le encargarán casos importantes. Conoce al dedillo todos los bares y prostíbulos del antiguo barrio chino. Es escéptico y en algunas cosas no ha cambiado nada: no soporta el asesinato cobarde, pero comprende a los pequeños delincuentes. No cree en la ley oficial, aunque sí en la de la calle.[8]

> (As a young man, Méndez, trained a thousand times in the basements of the Via Laietana police station, was an officer in the Francoist Criminal Brigade, but he took sandwiches to detained Communists and acted as their messenger. Now, the old cop works in the Nou de la Rambla station, at times they have confined him to the file room and he knows that he never will get promoted or be assigned important cases. He knows all the bars and brothels in the old red light district like the back of his hand. He is a sceptic and in some ways he has not changed a bit: he can't stand a cowardly murder, but he understands petty thieves. He doesn't believe in the official law, but he does believe in the law of the street.)

González Ledesma contemplates contemporary urban problems in his current novels. In *Una novela de barrio*, for example, Méndez observes the changes resulting from the neo-liberal, globalized world. Spain, and Barcelona, have become crossroads of cultures. The influx of immigrants has reduced regional identities and the rise of multinational corporations over regional industry has further obliterated Méndez's sense of place. The speculative boom in housing pushes traditional residents out of their homes, and Méndez himself no longer feels comfortable in his once familiar places. He nostalgically longs for the past, even though he realizes that the past was not an ideal world either. These sentiments closely recall those of Pepe Carvalho, and it appears that González Ledesma may be the most obvious candidate for the so-called doyen of Spanish crime fiction.

Eduardo Mendoza

Eduardo Mendoza is another writer who established himself during the Spanish transition to democracy and has continued writing crime fiction in the twenty-first century. Most well known for his comic parodies of crime fiction at the end of the 1970s, *El misterio de la cripta embrujada* (1979, The Mystery of the Enchanted Crypt) and *El laberinto de las aceitunas* (1982, The Olive Labyrinth), Mendoza revived his anonymous paranoid-schizophrenic investigator in 2001 with *La aventura del tocador de señoras* (The Adventure of the Ladies' Dressing Table). Like the detective characters of Manuel Vázquez Montalbán and Francisco González Ledesma, Mendoza's protagonist also has trouble adjusting to contemporary Barcelona. Newly released from the insane asylum where he has been confined for decades, Mendoza's investigator negotiates a city that has little to do with the place that he used to know. Nonetheless, he begins to create a new life for himself. The newly honourable and hard-working citizen is dragged back into the world of crime when he is obliged to steal a file from an office building. Subsequently, he becomes implicated in the murder of the executive whose office he robs and he must then solve the crime to clear his name. Mendoza consistently focuses on the corruption of Barcelona's upper class and the abuses that the rich heap upon the poor, and the author continually shows how the rich are unworthy of their privilege. Nonetheless, the corrupt system continues to assure the wealthy's hold on power, and Mendoza's investigator resigns himself to the struggle for a simple, uncomplicated life for himself and a few people around him.

Mendoza has published various additional novels during the last decade, but his role in Spanish crime fiction would have ended with *La aventura del tocador de señoras* if it had not been for the recent release of *El asombroso viaje de Pomponio Flato* (2008, The Amazing Journey of Pomponio Flato). Combining elements of crime fiction and the historical novel, Mendoza creates an unlikely story of a verbose, but ingenuous, Roman citizen travelling through the Middle East in the first century AD. In the village of Nazareth, he encounters the case of a carpenter who is condemned for the murder of a wealthy businessman.

The carpenter's son, Jesus, seeks Pomponio's help to clear his father's name, and the author adroitly weaves biblical references and other historical information into a sort of prequel to the Gospels. Despite the obvious disconnections with trends in crime fiction, Mendoza still reliably focuses on the *novela negra* tradition of unmasking the abuses of the wealthy and suffering of the underclass. Joseph is a victim of circumstance, and the official justice system will not be bothered to investigate the crime. Even when the truth is apparent, the real criminals never will be held accountable for their wrongdoings. Underscoring the advantages that members of the upper class enjoy over the poor, Mendoza includes a case of corrupt property development as motivation for powerful characters. Furthermore, the novel shows how Spanish authors are continuing to adapt the conventions of crime fiction to overlap with other rising genre fictions, such as the historical novel. More examples of these phenomena will become apparent as this survey of recent developments continues.

Following the historical pioneers

Veteran writers such as Manuel Vázquez Montalbán, Francisco González Ledesma and Eduardo Mendoza (among others) established the hard-boiled traditions of the Spanish *novela negra* in the 1970s and 1980s, and each continued a career into the twenty-first century. José Colmeiro would classify them as 'historical pioneers'.[9] Following in their footsteps is a group that Colmeiro has called 'die hards', or 'specialized writers who have opted for a closer and more faithful adaptation of the *roman noir* patterns, but carefully in tune with contemporary Spanish realities'.[10] One such author who has become relevant in the first decade of the twenty-first century is David Torres, who was the runner-up for the 2003 Nadal prize with his novel *El gran silencio* (The Big Silence).

David Torres (born in Madrid in 1966) was virtually unknown prior to his recognition as a Nadal finalist. *El gran silencio* connects to the traditions begun by Vázquez Montalbán and his generation who perceive crime fiction as a vehicle of social criticism. Torres places his characters in the same urban jungle of filth and suffering, showing a world of abuse and exploitation, seen through the eyes of a cynical, jaded observer who lives on the edge of the law but continually fights for his sense of justice.

Torres introduces a new type of protagonist in his novel: Roberto Esteban, a retired boxer. He is not a private detective, and does not work on cases. He does, however, move through the aforementioned scenes and atmospheres of the *novela negra* in which the members of the powerless underclass struggle to survive. Esteban's life story is fundamental to his current circumstances. He was a fair athlete in his prime, and he nearly achieved glory once by winning the European middleweight boxing championship. However, a brutal beating at the hands of a better Mexican fighter forced him to hang up his gloves and his downward spiral commenced.

As David Torres's hero is an ex-boxer, he clearly recalls Toni Romano, the protagonist in a series of novels by Juan Madrid, an early pioneer who has written few novels since the 1980s. These boxer characters struggle to make ends meet, often performing illegal tasks just to get by. However, Torres focuses on the sport itself, a topic that Madrid does not touch. *El gran silencio* includes a short history of boxing in Spain during the last decades, noting how boxers were exploited for entertainment when far less talented people were able to become rich and famous through vacuous celebrity or criminal corruption. Esteban cannot help but compare his humble background to those who have enjoyed privilege.

A further distinction sets Esteban apart from other Spanish crime fiction heroes. His last bout caused head injuries that steadily reduce his sense of hearing. He depends on lip reading while he sinks into the 'gran silencio' (big silence). Meanwhile, he collects recordings of Schumann's *Fantasy in C Major*, dedicating the last of his hearing to the notes of a musician who, according to legend, composed a masterpiece as he was going deaf. Torres continues the literary exploits of Roberto Esteban in a 2004 short story entitled 'El pequeño silencio' (The Little Silence) and he recently published another novel featuring the boxer entitled *Niños de tiza* (2008, Children of Chalk) in which Esteban reminisces about his childhood in San Blas in the 1980s. If, as is likely, Torres revisits this character, Roberto Esteban will stand as a die-hard follower of the traditions of hard-boiled social criticism of the Spanish *novela negra*.

While Torres is becoming known as a writer who innovates within the context of Spanish crime fiction, there are others who enter this arena without the intention of becoming identified as crime writers. Colmeiro describes these authors as 'recreational users, a considerable number of mainstream novelists who have occasionally approached the genre and introduced in their narratives specific motifs or formulas borrowed from the detective novel'.[11] One such recent example is Andrés Trapiello, who won the 2003 Nadal prize (over David Torres) for *Los amigos del crimen perfecto* (The Friends of the Perfect Crime). Andrés Trapiello (born in Manzaneda de Torío, León, in 1953) works as a journalist and essayist, and he is better known as a poet than a novelist. He has not written any similar works since winning the Nadal prize. Rather than subscribing to the conventions of *novela negra*, Trapiello's *Los amigos del crimen perfecto* relies on the tradition of the closed-room mystery, as few other recent Spanish crime novels do. The story revolves around a group of friends who meet weekly to discuss detective novels in Madrid's Café Comercial. They call their group 'Los Amigos del Crimen Perfecto', and with nicknames based on famous authors and characters (Poe, Marlowe, Miss Marple, Maigret, etc.), they muse on the 'perfect crime' as depicted in the stories they enjoy reading. The leader of the group is Paco Cortés, a hack author of cheap crime novels. Cortés (nicknamed Spade by the group) and several of his friends become implicated in the murder of the writer's father-in-law, an unpleasant police commissioner who was once a member of Franco's special police. They must clear themselves of the accusation, and when they are no longer under suspicion, they continue to investigate the crime in order to satisfy the taste for crime developed through their literary hobby.

Remembering the civil war

Trapiello's novel, while constituting crime fiction, also participates in a recent movement among Spaniards to remember events of the Spanish Civil War and the repression of the Franco regime. This trend is widely reported, even reaching the pages of the *New York Times* in November 2002:

> Suddenly, if episodically, Spain is waking from the collective amnesia that has paralyzed it for more than a quarter of a century. It was 1975 when Gen. Francisco Franco died, a monumental event in the country's history that brought to an end nearly four decades of dictatorship and ushered in an era of modern democratic rule. But only now is the country beginning to confront the terror of the 1936 army uprising and civil war that brought the generalissimo to power.[12]

Numerous critics, such as Teresa Vilarós and Joan Ramon Resina, have chronicled the collective memory loss and its cultural responses that Spaniards thought necessary to reach consensus during the transition to democracy of the 1970s and 1980s. Vilarós observes that works about the civil war began to appear in the mid-1990s, but the trend has become even more noticeable in Spain since the beginning of the twenty-first century, and numerous studies on this cultural phenomenon have appeared more recently.[13] While the 'recuperation of memory' and the reconsideration of the war's effects and aftermath is a general trend throughout Spanish cultural productions, the crime fiction genre does seem to have developed into a promising area to set stories about the civil war. The initial chapters of *Los amigos de crimen perfecto* coincide with the coup attempt that took place on 23 February 1981, when armed military officers entered the Spanish parliamentary chambers, fired shots into the ceiling and held the legislators hostage in an attempt to restore authoritarian rule. In this manner, the novel recalls the anxiety and fear that many accounts of the transition tend to overlook. As noted above, the characters investigate the murder of a police inspector who had worked as a member of Franco's secret police, zealously pursuing former Republicans in the post-war period. They discover that the crime was carried out by the son of a prisoner who had died in the custody of this same inspector many years earlier.

Very few Spanish writers have even hinted at this sort of reprisal against former Francoists for their crimes during and after the civil war. Nationalist retribution against Republicans was brutal (surely the reverse would have been true had the war ended differently). The desire for revenge probably weighed heavily on the minds of Republican sympathizers at the end of the regime, but Spain's unstated agreement for memory loss prevented many from reaching back to refuel their passions. While contemporaries of Trapiello have produced numerous histories of forgotten participants in the Spanish Civil War, his depiction of an actual act of vengeance is unique. At the end of the novel, the role of these resentments and fears among Spaniards – and their debate over the necessity of remembering – becomes a much more important topic than the actual crime and investigation. For Andrés Trapiello, then, the crime novel has become a useful vehicle for imagining latent emotions that may still lie deep within many of his fellow citizens.

Several other crime novels connect with the contemporary cultural focus on the Spanish Civil War. While it could be argued that virtually any account of the atrocities that characterize the war is an example of crime fiction, some notable examples illustrate how crime novels have expanded into this area. One such book is another Nadal prizewinner (2005), Pedro Zarraluki's *Un encargo difícil* (A Tough Assignment). Zarraluki is another 'recreational user', as he has been a noted novelist for several years, but he is not generally associated with crime fiction.

Additionally, he represents a recreational user broadening into areas beyond the traditional terrain of crime and investigation as it is written by authors who do not dedicate themselves wholly to the genre. *Un encargo difícil* is set in the war's immediate aftermath, when the wife of an executed Republican official is exiled with her daughter to the isolated Balearic island of Cabrera. The miserable island is home to few residents beyond some fishermen and a ragged military outpost. Despite her condition as a Republican widow, the islanders accept the woman and her daughter, and they live in relative harmony among the victors, making the best of primitive conditions on the island. The question of intrigue begins when a Francoist police inspector strands a German double agent on Cabrera in order to clean up a confusing political situation in Madrid. The island receives yet another resident when the inspector secretly obliges a former Republican prisoner to kill the German agent. Given the fairly dark circumstances of the plot development the novel surprises with a nearly comical account of the relationships among these various protagonists. The reluctant assassin and a befuddled military commander stumble their way to an acceptable outcome, making this text one of the more uplifting accounts of the war's aftermath.

A far darker novel, much more in line with expectations for an account of the Spanish Civil War, comes from Lorenzo Silva with *Carta blanca* (Carte Blanche), winner of the 2004 Primavera prize. Silva, a 'die hard' detective writer, is well known for his continuing series featuring the Guardia Civil sergeant Bevilacqua and corporal Chamorro, but he greatly expands the scope of his crime fiction by exploring the link between crime and war. The crimes of *Carta blanca* are true war atrocities. The first – a senseless campaign of plunder, rape and murder – is perpetrated by a squad of Spanish legionaries fighting in the Moroccan war in the 1920s. Silva documents the history of this conflict to create a graphic account of the Spanish army's policy of terrorizing the local population to punish its support of the anti-colonial insurgency. A decade later, one of these soldiers is fighting in the Republican defence of Badajoz. As he organizes a valiant but futile last stand against the brutal Nationalists (who are now supported by Moorish soldiers who rape and murder their Spanish enemies), he sees how the atrocities of battle become crimes only when the victors choose to pursue them as such. In reality, when soldiers are given carte blanche, there are no crimes in war. Potential witnesses disappear, leaving only the perpetrators themselves to remember such terrible events. As a result, there is no way to achieve any level of justice. Silva demonstrates a reality that recalls not only events of Spanish history, but also projects on to wars and atrocities in the present.

The depiction of the Spanish Civil War in crime fiction is a prime example of how this genre has expanded its scope with connections to topics that were largely beyond consideration before the twenty-first century. While crime writers did create a fairly wide array of topics on which to heap their social criticism, they tended to concentrate on the contemporary history of the democratic transition. In contrast, authors such as Trapiello, Zarraluki and Silva have used the genre to address additional episodes in the history of their country. These widening focuses diminish the currency of the 'die hard' or 'recreational user' labels, because their specific projects combine conventions of various types of fiction. In these cases, their novels take on additional roles as they participate in a developing cultural trend that expresses a once suppressed collective memory.

Gothic and the wider themes

A further illustration of how both genres and themes have expanded beyond their conventions and overlapped with many others in this decade is *La sombra del viento* (The Shadow of the Wind), the 2002 blockbuster novel by Carlos Ruiz Zafón. Set in post-civil war Barcelona, the characters live under the ominous influence of Francoist oppression. Nonetheless, the civil war themes are secondary to the labyrinthine plot and the setting of the city itself. Tiffany Gagliardi Trotman argues that Ruiz Zafón connects crime fiction with elements of Gothic fiction. The novel recreates a city of 'ruins, palaces, and cadavers, thereby reinforcing the dark backdrop in which the story unfolds'.[14] Since Daniel Sampere, the novel's protagonist, is a pre-teenaged boy (who comes of age during the story), it is difficult to link *La sombra del viento* to standards of detective fiction. However, the mysterious elements of the story, related to the search for information on the life of author Julián Carax, turn this book into an authentic novel of detection, even though it is not a detective story. Likewise, the multiple transgressions that Daniel uncovers make this work a novel about several crimes, rather than a crime novel that focuses on just one illegal act. As Daniel learns details about Carax and the people around him, the complicated plot mirrors the maze of dark streets and spaces through which they have both travelled. The Adlaya mansion, home of Carax's true love, is cast as the centre of the mystery, and the foreboding ruins of the old house are but one of the Gothic scenes that engage readers. More recently, Ruiz Zafón has published *El juego del Ángel* (2008, The Game of the Angel) with the same setting and a similar tone. With both novels, Zafón creates a complicated relationship among literary types and scenes in Spanish fiction today, to include crime fiction, the confrontation with the aftermath of the Spanish Civil War, Gothic fiction and the renewed interest in historical novels.

Spanish crime writers also consider more universal concerns. Many of these wide-ranging anxieties focus on the phenomenon that we now loosely define as 'globalization'. According to Josep Pont Vidal, Spaniards have coalesced in opposition to various facets of global culture, and he specifically highlights economic integration, reduction of labour rights around the world, immigration and ecological risks as topics that Spaniards have actively taken up since the 1990s.[15] We also could add a fear of political and economic hegemony to the list of commonly held anxieties over globalization. Rafael Reig (born in Asturias in 1963) engages nearly all of these fears by creating a fictional world in which the worst dreams of the anti-globalization movement have been realized. Two of Reig's novels, *Sangre a borbotones* (2002, Blood on the Saddle) and *Guapa de cara* (2004, A Pretty Face), reflect numerous Spanish and global concerns over energy, ecology, economy and culture.

Sangre a borbotones and *Guapa de cara* are two volumes that could become a series of postmodern accounts of postmodern Madrid. Although he relies fully on cultural familiarity with Spain's capital city, Reig rewrites recent history without shame. Necessary background information for understanding this world begins in 1979, when the entire world has exhausted its petroleum supplies. Madrid has flooded the city's main thoroughfares, so the former Paseo de la Castellana now is the Canal Castellana, and residents glide along in sailing boats. On smaller streets, bicycles are the main transportation. On either land or water, a driver's vehicle indicates his or her wealth. Not surprisingly, prestige and luxury is far beyond the budget of the average citizen. Luxurious areas of the city, particularly newly developed areas (called *recintos* (enclosed places)) in the north of the city, are reserved for the rich, while the poor are forcibly controlled in the *precintos* (sealed areas) in the south. Madrid is clearly divided into haves and have-nots, and it is no surprise that there are very few of the former and great masses of the latter.

The author does not show how the rest of the world, let alone the rest of Spain, deals with these circumstances. But additional events in Reig's historical version suggest numerous interactions among world powers. He writes that the Communist Party has taken control of the Spanish government following the failed coup attempt in February 1981. Reacting to the loss of a new democracy to communism, the United States has invaded Spain, which has then agreed to form the so called 'US-Iberian Federation'. There is little mention of government policies or controls in this system, but Spanish no longer is the dominant language of the land of Cervantes. The law requires that all citizens speak 'Anglo', and the use of Spanish, or even a Spanish accent in the speech of people a bit too old to learn the new language well, is another sign of social exclusion.

Reig may seem concerned with political and cultural hegemony, but governments do not control the world he portrays. Multinational corporations hold the real power, and the economy is at the service of the one that owns the most important information: the human genetic code. Chopeitia Genomics, a mysterious company that is rumoured to be allied with Telefónica (the Spanish national telephone company), is the true centre of power in Madrid. Within the towering pyramid of its corporate headquarters, Chopeitia's scientists perform unspeakable tests on human subjects, withholding the resulting discoveries until they can obtain the maximum return on their investment. Criminals are turned over to the laboratoriess for genetic experiments that advance the company's knowledge while disabling the victims for life. The chief of the company is Manex Chopeitia, an equally mysterious figure whom no living person has ever seen – or at least lived to report the sighting.

Reig presents this world in his 2002 novel *Sangre a borbotones*, which in turn introduces a new detective character. Carlos Clot is a down-on-his-luck private investigator who fulfills virtually every characteristic of his archetype. He charges 100 a day plus expenses, and gets 500 in advance. He has a small office on the thirteenth floor of the Torres Colón (The Columbus Towers), from which he views the traffic sailing by on the Canal Castellana when he is not busy with a client (which is most of the time). He is overweight, divorced, broke, poorly dressed and lives alone in a shabby apartment. His ex-wife now is married to a handsome, wealthy government and Telefónica official, and she prevents him from seeing their daughter. Clot frequently braces himself with a bottle of whisky kept in his filing cabinet; serving himself whatever the time of day. *Guapa de cara* is the second novel set in this terrible version of the

Spanish capital. In each of these stories, Clot discovers that Chopeitia is behind all the crimes he investigates, but he is powerless to stop the manipulation and corruption. Reig's version of Madrid is bleak but, for many residents, contemporary life in this city is nearly as hard, completely within the tradition of hard-boiled *novela negra*.

A final reality of Spanish crime fiction in this decade has been its complete integration within the commercial apparatus of the publishing industry. Long considered a form of low-brow popular culture, detective novels, along with their writers and readers, are no longer relegated to the margins of the literary establishment. However, this enhanced prestige has meant that authors and their stories are now turned into commodities, as books have become just another consumer good. There are numerous accounts of the ways that market interests are now more important than concerns about literary quality, and it seems that books are now presented as just anything else sold to the public. An author who becomes too successful commercially, then, often risks the rejection of those who would hold literary standards above market concerns. Anne Walsh quotes Alfonso Ruiz de Aguirre to summarize these circumstances: 'escribir bien y vender mucho es un pecado mortal que los supuestos vigilantes de la calidad literaria no pueden consentir' (to write well and sell a lot is a mortal sin which the supposed vigilantes of literary quality cannot allow).[16]

A new focus on controversy – Víctor Saltero

If, indeed, the conscious marketing of an author provokes debates over literary quality in Spain, a writer who calls himself Víctor Saltero is a new focal point in the controversy. With four texts, three of which are detective novels, released since spring 2007 by a new publishing house that is dedicated solely to his work, Saltero's emergence has surprised in numerous ways. On one hand, it is hardly typical for a writer to produce so many texts in so little time and, on the other, this unusual productivity has provoked a strong reaction – frequently approaching incredulity – among observers.

There is little to write on Saltero's background, because the name is a pseudonym for someone who wishes to remain anonymous. Abundant conjecture about his identity has shed little light on the mystery. Writing in *El Mundo*, Quico Alsedo cites speculation that 'se trata de un primer espada del mundo de los negocios con veleidades literarias' (the author is an important leader in the business world who has hidden literary aspirations) while bloggers on cultural websites (who also remain rather anonymous) have wondered if the author is really a committee of writers.[17] Jesús Ruiz Mantilla reports that the editor of Imser Siglo, Saltero's publisher, has revealed only 'que es empresario, que no tiene problemas de dinero, que escribía por afición' (he is a businessman, who does not have any financial problems, who writes because he likes to).[18] Saltero does not appear in public, nor does he grant interviews. Other than the published novels, the only concrete sign of life has been an e-mailed reply to questions from *La Nación* journalist Begoña Marín, but she notes that he was extremely careful not to reveal any information that would identify him.[19]

Saltero's contribution to detective fiction in Spain lies in three novels: *Sucedió en el AVE* (2007, It Happened on the High Speed Train), *El amante de la belleza* (2007, The Lover of Beauty) and *Sucedió en la Moncloa* (2008, It Happened in the Moncloa Palace). *Sucedió en el AVE* introduces the characters who populate Saltero's crime series: Quintero, a veteran police inspector in Seville, and an acquaintance, Víctor Saltero, a former attorney whose professional success now allows him an impossibly sybaritic lifestyle in which he writes crime novels. The plot unfolds rather simply, always guided by Quintero's gruff and tough demeanour and Saltero's brilliant analysis and conclusions. The pair represent the opposite poles in crime fiction characters: the hard-boiled detective versus the intellectual, logical sleuth. The enigma in these novels is minimized because the narrator frequently shifts perspectives to describe the crime itself. Readers, then, become cheerleaders, hoping that the police inspector and his friend are able to perceive and unravel the fairly obvious clues before them. In this story, they investigate the murder of two former ETA terrorists on the high speed train from Madrid to Seville. The narrator reveals the killer's identity early in the story: a young man who witnessed the two Basques assassinating his older brother, a police officer in a northern Spanish town. With this theme, *Sucedió en el AVE* connects on a visceral level with current events in Spain: the history of Basque separatism, recent terrorist attacks and controversy over the government's secret negotiations with ETA. The novel takes the side of the majority of Spaniards who resent terrorist violence. Once Quintero and Saltero uncover the truth behind the shootings, they pursue justice by devising a convincing legal explanation to absolve the killer – despite several witnesses who could tell the truth if they chose to do so. The novel thus expresses a popular sentiment in Spain, which was confirmed with a poll on the book's official website. Nearly 75 per cent of respondents to the question '¿Y tú qué harías: encubrirías o delatarías?' (What would you do: report or stay silent?) would not reveal the murderer's identity. Whether they call this a case of revenge or of justice, most Spaniards express understanding of – if not empathy for – the murderer.

The case of *El amante de la belleza* takes Quintero and Saltero to Barcelona, where they investigate the disappearances of a female teacher and a female student in a secondary school. The two go missing in separate incidents, and the crimes are seemingly completely unrelated. For the reader, again, the mystery is minimal. The novel narrates both abductions, and we have an uncomfortable window on the life of a seemingly mild-mannered school teacher who has singled out these two women for their physical beauty. Before snatching them off the street by offering them a lift on a rainy day, the kidnapper has prepared a luxurious underground residence in which he imprisons the captives, admiring their beauty via closed-circuit video cameras hidden in their rooms. The women are cut off from the rest of the world, and the 'amante de la belleza' keeps them for his own viewing pleasure (somewhat surprisingly, the kidnapper's motivation is not sexual – he is satisfied with watching the women from his control room). The readers know all of this information, and once again we are aware of the clues and hope that Saltero will correctly guide Quintero towards resolution.

Saltero's relationship with a new publishing house and its unprecedented marketing campaign have distracted from discussions of the literary merits of these novels. As reported by Jesús Ruiz Mantilla, Saltero had sold some 100,000 novels by December 2007, an impressive sum for any Spanish author, let alone for a previously unknown writer who does not collaborate with public appearances, signings or interviews. These numbers are even more remarkable for a new publisher dedicated to a single author. According to reports, Imser Siglo was created by a group of Spanish businessmen, only two of whom have identified themselves publicly. The motives for this commercial arrangement also are unclear but, clearly, the group has a credible business plan. *Sucedió en el AVE* was rolled out with an unprecedented media campaign, which included poster advertisements in city metros and bus stops, radio spots and full-page newspaper advertisements. These promotions were unlike any other literary publicity seen in Spain, and the advertising undoubtedly increased sales. But the reasons for success are probably more complicated. Could the novel's hinting at taking revenge on ETA terrorists resonate with the reading public? Was the promotion of a new author enough to call attention to the novel? Was the novel really good? The subsequent release of *El amante de la belleza*, so soon after the first novel by Saltero appeared, supplied abundant material for critics, who opened savage attacks over the quality of these novels.

Critics have been harsh with Saltero. Rafael Reig poses some questions that leave no doubt about his own assessment of the novel: '¿Por qué dedicar tanto dinero a promocionar una novela mala? ¿Es que no tenían a mano nada mejor? ¿Por qué no buscar una novela al menos tolerable?' (Why did they spend so much money on advertising a bad novel? Didn't they have anything better? Why not look for a novel that's at least tolerable?)[20] The sales of Saltero's novel, he believes, are entirely the result of the marketing campaign. Other critics, such as Vicente Verdú, have joined Reig in dismissing these novels and lamenting their effects on contemporary Spanish literature and culture.[21] In the end, the works of Víctor Saltero inspire more discussion on commercial publishing in Spain than they ever will on crime fiction.

Conclusion

To conclude this examination of Spanish crime fiction of the first decade of this century, it appears that the genre is alive and well, and that there is no reason to believe that it is nearing an end, despite the fact that 'early pioneers' are ageing or have already passed away. We have seen that these pioneer writers have continued their craft, extending their established practices in creative manners that continue to attract attention to their new titles. Younger writers have found inspiration in the pioneers, adopting traditional conventions and becoming even more 'die hard' authors than their elders. Other writers have entered the crime fiction arena, some as 'casual practitioners', but with much more to say about topics and themes that seem to find the detective novel an ideal vehicle to articulate their stories. These topics have widened the reach of the traditional *novela negra*, and now crime novels consider nearly any relevant social concern in contemporary Spain. And given Spain's presence in globalized world culture, commercial practices of marketing will shape further developments in these works. With the integration of detective novels into national debates and globalized business, we can see that Spanish crime fiction has become a mainstream cultural product even as it perpetuates the features of popular fiction that once marginalized the practice.

* * *

Extract from *El Gran Silencio* (The Big Silence) by David Torres

Roberto Esteban is visiting his mother in his childhood neighbourhood of San Blas.

'OK,' I said, leaving the glass in the sink. 'I have to go now.'

'Already, son?'

I shrugged my shoulders. Every time I came over to my mother's on Sunday, I ran out of words half way through lunch. We never had a lot to say to each other, and the mute reproach of her eyes, the walls of silence between each spoonful, her quick steps to the kitchen to clear away a bowl or bring the salt shaker, none of that mattered more than the fact that she was my mother and I was her only child. Maybe I wasn't a good son, but that's how things were. Those unexpressed complaints piled up in the same mail room where they store letters without a return address, right next to the invitations we turn down, the women we walk by at the bar, the low blows and the drawn matches.

I kissed her cheek and went outside. The four o'clock sun hit me right in the face, blinding me for a few seconds. A stray dog came up to smell my shoes, and I kicked him away. The sunlight shone down on the whitewashed walls of that row of poor houses that had been the setting of my childhood. A pavement covered in dog shit, a forest of television antennas, thin partitions beside which I sat to hear the neighbours' arguments. During my brief boxing career I hadn't won enough money to buy my parents the mansion that I had promised myself I would give them some day: a two-storey house with a real garden, swimming pool, guard dog and a tall iron fence, just like the houses on Arturo Soria where my mother went to drop off her dresses. When I was just a boy, I liked going with her, getting on the crowded bus while my mother held the package of her delicately folded work tightly to her chest. I was just a kid, but on those trips, I got to see the subtle border that the bus crossed every time it passed by the Cross of the Fallen monument: the expensive cars, the manicured lawns, the scent of eucalyptus and lavender, the trees that generously shaded the streets. The children didn't even play with the same cheap, faded toys that the kids in my neighbourhood played with: they didn't have little plastic cars or wooden swords, but radio-controlled cars and air rifles, and years later, in the outdoor summer bars, I smelled expensive perfumes, I saw the different quality of their clothes, the brilliant skin of rich young women, and the shine of feminine hair when it has grown without worrying about anything more than looking like silk.

Jealousy? Yeah, I suppose so. You can think whatever you like. I looked at my mother's grey hair and her hands, broken down by sewing and years of washing with home-made soap, thinking of the injustice of being born in a neighbourhood without gardens or fences, a neighbourhood bordered by an empty lot littered with rubble crawling with spiders and lizards, the smell of cooked cabbage in the doorways, the bars full of people at all hours, always full of taciturn men who drank beer after beer in a malignant silence, and women who were going home after scrubbing stairways all day.

Back then, I didn't even know that there was something called unemployment. If they sent me to the tavern to buy white wine, I always looked at the calendar that had a spectacular blonde smiling at me from some other world, while I felt the stares of all of those wine-clouded eyes on the back of my head. Time went by and the calendar girls changed, they changed bikinis or hairstyles, they were redheads or brunettes, they wore fine lingerie or were naked, but they didn't get older, they didn't die, they didn't complain. That was their job: to make the men who drank alone in the taverns or blackened their hands with grease in a mechanic's garage happy. In contrast, the eyes that gazed over the golden mirages of the calendars were always the same, empty, bloodshot, shaky, just like the hands that held onto a beer as time passed by. Years later, I understood that unemployment had ruined a whole generation in my neighbourhood, the same way that syringes and spoons took most of the next one, or cirrhosis took my father.

When I was walking by the pensioners' social centre that they had built on the empty lot where I used to play, I was struck by a spurious memory: for a moment, I thought that the spiders that lived in the old, crumbling wall where we hunted them down with sticks still were living in the gaps in the bricks. Three old men were sitting in the sun on a bench, next to one of the walls. The middle one raised his cane in a vague sign of recognition, as if he were shooing away a wasp. I waved back and then he raised his hand, waving me closer.

'Esteban?' he asked, with a cough. 'Are you Roberto Esteban?'

I nodded. The old man mumbled something to his friends, something like 'See, I told you so', and hit the sand with his cane.

'Are you sure you're Esteban? The boxer, Nati's boy?'

'Do I know you?' I asked, sorry that I'd paid attention to him.

'You don't remember me,' the old man said shaking his head. 'You don't remember. Your father and I were friends. Salvador.'

I looked at that old, wrinkled face, so much like the pot scrubbers that my mother insisted on using until they fell apart in her hands. I looked at the flabby mouth, held up by his dentures, and his eyes lost in a mountain of spider webs, but I didn't find anything, not the slightest sign that tied him to my past. He wasn't anything more than an anonymous old man in a beret, perfectly interchangeable with any other old man in the neighbourhood, with any of the friends that kept him company.

'Salvador, of course.' I said. 'How are things?'

'How are things?' he mumbled in a mixture of exclamation, question and reply. 'Just like the neighbourhood.'

'Sure,' I said, and I shook the hand that he had been holding out with the patience of an old spider. 'I'm glad to see you.'

I was walking down the street when I saw that the old man was waving his cane again. I went back because it looked like he wanted to say something to me. Either that or his dentures had come loose. The old man moved his mouth slowly and his words seemed to float right in front of his face.

'What ever happened to you?' I finally understood him. 'What ever happened to you in all these years?'

David Torres, *El gran silencio* (Barcelona: Destino, 2003), pp. 13–18. Translated by David Knutson.

Notes

[1] Eduardo Mendoza, 'Telonero' [Understudy], *El País*, 27 October 2003, 88.
[2] Caragh Wells, 'Urban dialectics in Vázquez Montalbán', *Forum for Modern Language Studies*, XL (January 2004), 83–95
[3] José V. Saval, *Manuel Vázquez Montalbán. El triunfo de un luchador incansable* [Manuel Vázquez Montalbán. The Triumph of a Tireless Fighter] (Madrid: Síntesis, 2004), p. 220.
[4] Ibid.
[5] Carlos Geli, 'En España todavía falta cultura lectora para la novela negra' [Spain still lacks reading culture for *novela negra*], *El País*, 8 September 2007, 42.
[6] Ibid.
[7] Ibid.
[8] Rosa Mora, 'El recuperado Méndez' [Méndez recovered], *El País*, 5 February 2007, 50.
[9] José F. Colmeiro, 'The Spanish connection: detective fiction after Franco', *Journal of Popular Culture*, 28, 1 (summer 1994), 153.
[10] Ibid.
[11] Ibid., 151–61.
[12] E. Sciolino and E. Daly, 'Spaniards at last confront the ghost of Franco', *New York Times*, 11 November 2002, A3.
[13] Teresa Vilarós, *El mono del desencanto. Una crítica cultural de la transición española (1973–1993)* [The Hangover of the Dissillusionment. A Cultural Criticism of the Spanish Transition] (Madrid: Siglo XXI, 1998), p. 4.
[14] Tiffany Gagliardi Trotman, 'Haunted *noir*: neo-Gothic Barcelona in Carlos Ruiz Zafón's *La sombra del viento*', *Romance Studies*, 25, 4 (November 2007), 269–77.
[15] Josep Pont Vidal, *La ciudadanía se moviliza. Los movimientos sociales y la globalización en España* [The Citizens Mobilize. Social Movements and Globalization in Spain] (Barcelona: Flor de Viento, 2004).

16 Anne L. Walsh, *Arturo Pérez-Reverte: Narrative Tricks and Narrative Strategies* (Woodbridge: Tamesis, 2007), p. 13.
17 Quico Alsedo, 'Mundo Ficción llevará al cine la segunda novela de Víctor Saltero' [Mundo Ficción will film the second novel of Víctor Saltero], *El Mundo*, 22 May 2007, 64.
18 Jesús Ruiz Mantilla, 'La era de los escritores fantasma' [The era of the ghost writers], *El País*, 17 December 2007, 44.
19 Begoña Marín, '¿Quién se oculta tras Víctor Saltero?' [Who is hiding behind Víctor Saltero?], *La Nación*, 26 April 2008, *http://www.lanacion. es/?p=4291*.
20 Rafael Reig, 'El "efecto Saltero": Que nos den más "chopped", por favor' [The Saltero effect: may we have more 'chopped', please?], *El Mundo*, 30 April 2007, 39.
21 Vicente Verdú, 'El marketing cultural del tocomocho' [Cultural marketing of the shell game], *El País*, 3 May 2007, 45.

Bibliography

Alsedo, Quico, 'Mundo Ficción llevará al cine la segunda novela de Víctor Saltero' [Mundo Ficción will film the second novel of Víctor Saltero], *El Mundo*, 22 May 2007, 64.

Colmeiro, José F., 'The Spanish connection: detective fiction after Franco', *Journal of Popular Culture*, 28, 1 (summer 1994), 151–61.

——, 'The Hispanic (dis)connection: some leads and a few missing links', *Journal of Popular Culture*, 34, 4 (spring 2001), 49–64.

Gagliardi Trotman, Tiffany, 'Haunted *noir*: neo-Gothic Barcelona in Carlos Ruiz Zafón's *La sombra del viento*', *Romance Studies*, 25, 4 (November 2007), 269–77.

Geli, Carlos, 'En España todavía falta cultura lectora para la novela negra' [Spain still lacks reading culture for *novela negra*], *El País*, 8 September 2007, 42.

González Ledesma, F., *Crónica sentimental en rojo* [Sentimental Chronicle in Red] (Barcelona: Planeta, 1984).

——, *La dama de Cachemira* [The Cashmere Lady] (Barcelona: Planeta, 1986).

——, *El pecado o algo parecido* [Sin, or Something Like It] (Madrid: Planeta, 2002).

——, *Una novela de barrio* [A Neighbourhood Novel] (Barcelona: RBA, 2007).

Marín, Begoña, '¿Quién se oculta tras Víctor Saltero?', *La Nación*, 26 April 2008, *http://www.lanacion.es/?p=4291*, viewed 16 June 2008.

Mendoza, Eduardo, *El misterio de la cripta embrujada* [The Mystery of the Enchanted Crypt] (Barcelona: Seix Barral, 1979).

——, *El laberinto de las aceitunas* [The Olive Labyrinth] (Barcelona: Seix Barral, 1982).

———, *La aventura del tocador de señoras* [The Adventure of the Ladies' Dressing Table] (Barcelona: Seix Barral, 2001).

———, 'Telonero' [Understudy], *El País*, 27 October 2003, 88.

———, *El asombroso viaje de Pomponio Flato* [The Amazing Journey of Pomponio Flato] (Barcelona: Seix Barral, 2008).

Mora, Rosa, 'El recuperado Méndez' [Méndez recovered] *El País*, 5 February 2007, 50.

Pont Vidal, Josep, *La ciudadanía se moviliza. Los movimientos sociales y la globalización en España* [The Citizens Mobilize. Social Movements and Globalization in Spain] (Barcelona: Flor de Viento, 2004).

Reig, Rafael, *Sangre a borbotones* [Blood on the Saddle] (Madrid: Lengua de Trapo, 2002).

———, *Guapa de cara* [A Pretty Face] (Madrid: Lengua de Trapo, 2004).

———, 'El "efecto Saltero": Que nos den más "chopped," por favor' [Who is Hiding Behind Víctor Saltero?], *El Mundo*, 30 April 2007, 39.

Resina, Joan Ramon, 'Short of memory: the reclamation of the past since the Spanish transition to democracy', in his *Disremembering the Dictatorship: The Politics of Memory in the Spanish Transition to Democracy* (Amsterdam and Atlanta: Rodopi, 2000), pp. 83–126.

Ruiz Mantilla, Jesús, 'La era de los escritores fantasma' [The Era of the Ghost Writers], *El País*, 17 December 2007, 44.

Ruiz Zafón, Carlos, *La sombra del viento* [The Shadow of the Wind] (Barcelona: Planeta, 2002).

———, *El juego del Ángel* [The Game of the Angel] (Barcelona: Planeta, 2008).

Saltero, Víctor, *El amante de la belleza* [The Lover of Beauty] (Madrid: Imser Siglo, 2007).

———, *Sucedió en el AVE* [It Happened on the High Speed Train] (Madrid: Imser Siglo, 2007).

———, *Sucedió en la Moncloa* [It Happened in the Moncloa Palace] (Madrid: Imser Siglo, 2008).

Saval, José V., *Manuel Vázquez Montalbán. El triunfo de un luchador incansable* [Manuel Vázquez Montalbán. The Triumph of a Tireless Fighter] (Madrid: Síntesis, 2004).

Sciolino, E. and E. Daly, 'Spaniards at last confront the ghost of Franco', *New York Times*, 11 November 2002, A3.

Silva, Lorenzo, *Carta blanca* [Carte Blanche] (Madrid: Espasa-Calpe, 2004).

Trapiello, Andrés, *Los amigos del crimen perfecto* [The Perfect Crime Club] (Barcelona: Destino, 2003).

Torres, David, *El gran silencio* [The Big Silence] (Barcelona: Destino, 2003).

———, 'Un pequeño silencio' [The Little Silence], *Prótesis. Publicación consagrada al crimen*, 3 April 2004, 28–31.

———, *Niños de tiza* [Children of Chalk] (Sevilla: Algaida, 2008).

Vázquez Montalbán, Manuel, *Milenio Carvalho I. Rumbo a Kabul* [Carvalho Millennium I. On the Road to Kabul] (Barcelona: Planeta, 2004).

——, *Milenio Carvalho II. En las Antípodas* [Carvalho Millennium II. In the Antipodes] (Barcelona: Planeta, 2004).
——, *Tatuaje* [Tattoo] (Barcelona: José Batalló, 1974).
Verdú, Vicente, 'El marketing cultural del tocomocho' [Cultural Marketing of the Shell Game], *El País*, 3 May 2007, 45.
Vilarós, Teresa M., *El mono del desencanto. Una crítica cultural de la transición española (1973–1993)* [The Hangover of the Dissillusionment. A Cultural Criticism of the Spanish Transition] (Madrid: Siglo XXI, 1998).
Walsh, Anne L., *Arturo Pérez-Reverte: Narrative Tricks and Narrative Strategies* (Woodbridge: Tamesis, 2007).
Wells, Caragh, 'Urban dialectics in Vázquez Montalbán', *Forum for Modern Language Studies*, XL (January 2004), 83–95.
Zarraluki, Pedro, *Un encargo difícil* [A Tough Assignment] (Barcelona: Destino, 2005).

7
Five Cases from 130 Years of Portuguese Detective Fiction, 1870s–2000s

PAUL M. CASTRO

It has become a commonplace to approach any evaluation of Portuguese detective fiction by first referring to the genre's paucity of tradition in Portugal.[1] Yet, whilst the development of detective fiction has been intermittent, the genre does have a relatively long history in the country. Another aspect of the attention devoted to the detective fiction genre on the part of lusitanists is the tendency to focus on the appropriation of aspects of the genre by mainstream literary fiction.[2] In this chapter I shall instead try to sketch out the main lines of Portuguese detective fiction avowedly written for a popular audience between 1870 and the turn of the twenty-first century, concentrating on works that are invaluable to the understanding of the history and evolution of the detective story within Portugal, but which remain largely unknown elsewhere.

Within the period in question, as Orlando Guerra points out, Portuguese detective fiction grew fitfully in reaction to literary developments abroad and the political situation at home.[3] In his article Guerra provides a useful list of the main practitioners of the genre in Portugal, yet rarely goes beyond one- or two-line descriptions of individual works. Here I have preferred to provide an extended discussion of five main cases: the first Portuguese work that can be described as detective fiction; the first dedicated Portuguese detective fiction novelist; the most successful Portuguese detective fiction novelist; the prize that resuscitated detective fiction in Portugal after the fall of the dictatorship and which set the scene for the establishment and maturation of the genre in the 1990s; and, finally, the author who best represents the result of this process of development.

Eça de Queiroz's and Ramalho Ortigão's
O Mistério da Estrada de Sintra *(1870)*

For Orlando Guerra, 'the publication in 1870 of *O Mistério da Estrada de Sintra* (The Sintra Road Mystery) is considered almost unanimously as marking the appearance of the detective novel in Portugal'.[4] First published as a feuilleton in the newspaper *Diário de Notícias*, to some extent this work sets the tone for the future development of the genre in the country. *O Mistério* was written by Eça de Queiroz in conjunction with Ramalho Ortigão, although, according to Ernesto Guerra da Cal, Queiroz composed the lion's share of the narrative.[5] Both writers were involved at the time with what were known as the *Conferências do Casino*, a series of symposia held to diagnose the social and political ills then affecting the Iberian Peninsula and to suggest procedures for effecting a national renaissance in Portugal. Queiroz, who presented a paper on realist fiction, would subsequently go on to become Portugal's greatest realist writer. It may, therefore, seem strange that he would begin his career with *O Mistério*, a work so overblown that it veers from elaborate flourishes typical of the romantic literature that the *conferencistas* were bent on overturning to a Gothic creepiness, interspersed with interludes of fantasy and jolts of adventure. For Eça and Ramalho, however, there was a critical method underlying what initially appears to be the novel's overblown romanticism.

O Mistério was essentially designed as a hoax, a spoof devised to reveal the attitudes of its readers and expose their stance to critical ridicule. It was, in effect, the first instance of the playfulness that has often characterized the detective fiction genre in Portugal. Even at its most hard boiled, 'tongue' is not usually far from 'cheek' in Portuguese detective fiction. For critic Ofélia Paiva Monteiro, Eça de Queiroz and Ramalho Ortigão intended to test the credulousness of a Portuguese public, whose critical perception of the real had been dulled by excesses of romanticism, and reveal the extent to which it could be stretched before it snapped.[6] Eça and Ramalho, both friends of the editor of the *Diário de Notícias*, had the innovative and unprecedented idea of passing off the narrative as a real event, related in the form of a series of letters to the editor from readers themselves involved in the mystery. Putatively, due to restrictions on space, Eça and Ramalho had the story printed in the space usually reserved for the feuilleton. The day before the first instalment of *O Mistério* began, the editor of *Diário de Notícias* published a notice declaring that he had received a letter, a 'stupendous narration', recounting tales of kidnap and murder, and that it would be published verbatim, due to its 'interest' and 'literary quality', in the space usually reserved for the feuilleton.

This tactic created what Ramalho later termed the 'romance noticiário', a 'news novel', a 'feuilleton such as neither the French nor the Americans had yet managed to invent'.[7] By dint of a presentation of events within an epistolary framework, interspersed with references to real places, successive letters confirming diegetic details, and the narrative's juxtaposition with items of real news, the (ironically) rocambolesque events of the mystery were given a veneer of actuality that should have been stripped away by the obviously artificial events. As well as the manifest clue contained in its compositional placement, the narrative itself contains many allusive 'winks' to the reader of the time. The narrator expresses regret for the 'Ponson du Terail' quality of his narrative; some characters praise the 'spirit of novelistic adventure' of other characters and so forth. Eça and Ramalho's bluff worked. In a way now reminiscent of the effects of Orson Welles's radiophonic adaptation of *War of the Worlds*, the public were taken in by the deception, and frightened citizens began to avoid the road to Sintra, a prosaic carriageway that became draped with an air of mystery.

The first letter, signed Doutor ***, begins by entreating the editor of the *Diário de Notícias* to print the current missive in the hope that one of the newspaper's readers might be able to help solve the mystery. Doutor *** relates how he and his companion had been waylaid by masked men on the road between Sintra and Lisbon. These men, who were 'obviously gentlemen', then blindfolded the doctor and took him to examine a dead man, who appeared to have taken an overdose of opium. This section of the narrative is dense with mystery and is highly confusing. The doctor does not know who is dead or who the murderer is, nor does he know the identity of his kidnappers or the identity of the mysterious man.

The subsequent letters deepen the mystery until the kidnapper himself writes a letter to put the record straight. His letter recounts the past story of the dead man, who was an English officer named Rytmel, and describes the officer's colourful affair with the Countess W (who is the letter writer's cousin) in an account involving fiery Cuban lovers, a flight from Malta by yacht, tiger hunts and deadly duels. The story is flushed with sentimentality and incongruous adventure. The final letter relates the confession of Countess W. We learn of her frustrated romance, her jealousy at the possibility of Rytmel's being amorously attached to an Irishwoman named Miss Shaw. We learn that Countess W. had drugged Rytmel with the intention of ransacking his correspondence in search of a compromising letter from Miss Shaw. The Countess inadvertently gave Rytmel a mortal overdose. She found no letter.

It is really only in the letter from the doctor (and to a lesser extent the letters from Z. and A.M.C.) that the protagonist can be deemed the investigator. The doctor searches the house for clues, and tries to work out the circumstances of Rytmel's death from details such as the absence of his tie (which no gentleman would have gone out without wearing). The doctor learns that Rytmel had £2,300 in cash, prompting the important question of the current whereabouts of the money. The suicide note is rather implausible and has a female hair attached to it (it reads 'I declare I have killed myself with Opium'), and it turns out to be a forgery. In this section the doctor is the detective. At the end of his letter, however, he explicitly cedes this position to the newspaper readers and retires from the scene. Rather than the doctor's interpellating suspects or searching out the masked men, it is the reader himself who hears new testimonies in each instalment. It is now the suspects and the interviewees who volunteer information and thus, seemingly, control the pace of the mystery's revelation. Todorov theorized a well-known twofold narrative structure to detective fiction, the story of the murder alongside the story of the investigation that reconstructs the crime. In the 'romance-noticiário', the revelation of the 'investigation' takes place in the real time of letters to a newspaper. These testimonies are presented to the hypothetical newspaper reader, making the public the detective. This places the newspaper readers in a position of critical authority, a control that Eça and Ramalho wanted them to exercise by reacting to and ultimately rejecting the artificiality of the story (however much they may have enjoyed it).

O Mistério introduces two characteristics that would recur in Portuguese detective fiction: a close attachment to the world of journalism and crime reporting; and the inchoate use of the detective model to criticize the nation (here in so far as the novel condemns the Portuguese public's attachment to an outmoded Romanticism). Eça's and Ramalho's story inaugurates the proto-period of Portuguese detective fiction. Other detective novels published at around the same period include those of Francisco Leite Bastos (the first Portuguese writer to have dedicated himself to writing something approximating detective fiction), Fialho de Almeida (another *conferencista*) and João Chagas, though none of their works improved upon *O Mistério*, or indeed went beyond copying Eça's and Ramalho's points of reference: the works of Poe, Gaboriau and Eugène Sue.

Repórter X's O Táxi no.9297 *(1926)*

If *O Mistério da Estrada de Sintra* was the first work of detective fiction, the first true writer of detective fiction was Reinaldo Ferreira, later to be better known as Repórter X. Orlando Guerra divides the history of the detective novel in the early twentieth century into two rough periods, one between 1900 and 1930 and another between 1930 and the Second World War. This division is not, however, attributed to any specific detail or development. Furthermore, he writes that the second period was 'animated by the pen and imagination and dynamism of Reinaldo Ferreira, the unforgettable Repórter X'.[8] Reinaldo Ferreira was a contemporary and comrade of the writers of the Futurist generation that Guerra includes in the first period, such as Fernando Pessoa and Sá-Carneiro.[9] Since he was publishing his work in the 1920s and in the 1930s (up until his death in 1935) alongside the writers that Guerra places in the second epoch of Portuguese detective fiction, it would seem appropriate to count this as one period and to consider Reinaldo Ferreira as its tutelary figure.

Reinaldo Ferreira was one of the most mercurial cultural figures of his turbulent age. It was a time of upheaval and instability, characterized by high profile assassinations, audacious frauds, lurid crimes and outrageous scandals, and encompassed the imposition of military rule in 1928 and the establishment of the *Estado Novo* in 1933. Apart from his intrepid reporting, Ferreira made his name with sensational reports of sordid crimes written under the name of Repórter X. Ferreira's pseudonym was created when a hastily scrawled 'Reynaldo F' was misunderstood as 'Repórter X' by a typesetter. Ferreira liked the effect so much that he adopted the name as his *nom de guerre*.

Repórter X's popularity as a writer of detective novellas never faltered in his lifetime. Prominent amongst his works are *Preto e Branco* (1923, Black and White), *O Táxi no.9297* (1926, Taxi 9297) and *A Virgem do Bristol Club* (1930, The Bristol Club Virgin). Repórter X's novellas featured a variety of detectives, some Portuguese and some American. Whilst the early detective fiction had no qualms about translating foreign models into Portuguese terms, as the genre developed it became more and more common to use detectives and settings from abroad. For the most part, however, Repórter X's investigators and locations were Portuguese. One detective in particular, journalist Gil Goes, proved a big hit with readers upon the publication of the narrative in which he featured, *O Mistério de Rua Saraiva de Carvalho* (The Saraiva de Carvalho Road Mystery). In the introduction to the 1974 edition of *O Táxi no.9297*, we are told that this feuilleton 'enthralled Lisbon as had *O Mistério da Estrada de Sintra* half a century before'.[10] Many of Repórter X's stories feature himself as the detective, and the approximation of detection to reportage seems to be a recurrent theme in both his fiction and his journalism, perpetuating this line in the evolution of Portuguese detective fiction.

With the installation of the *Estado Novo* dictatorship and the development in the literature of the period of the more sober, issue-focused and political neo-realism, Repórter X was largely forgotten as a writer until the 1960s. Then the advent of external artistic currents more attuned to a popular sensibility accompanied a change in attitudes that meant the demotic, escapist writings of Repórter X were again viewed with approval. As well as being one of the first successful writers of detective fiction of his time, Repórter X was also one of the first Portuguese writers to reflect on the genre, notably in his article 'Existe literatura policial entre nós? Havia vantagens e desvantagens em a criar em Portugal?' (Does crime literature exist amongst us? Would there be advantages or disadvantages to creating it in Portugal?) published in 1918.[11]

The most representative Repórter X novella is *O Táxi no.9297* (Taxi 9297), published in 1926, the year in which democracy in Portugal was dismantled. The plot is loosely based on the murder of a Portuguese actress named Maria Alves, which Repórter X had covered for his paper. Like the murdered actress in *O Táxi no.9297*, Maria Alves's corpse was found lying face down at the side of a street in Lisbon. As in *O Táxi no.9297*, the first hypothesis is that the actress had been murdered by a gang of thieves. Repórter X, the journalist, does not credit this version of events. After carrying out some background investigation, Repórter X expounds through his column the hypothesis that the murder had been committed by Maria Alves's impresario, Augusto Gomes. Repórter X also suggests that Gomes may have murdered his first wife and one of his lovers as well. Although these earlier crimes have never been proven, the police have collected enough evidence to arrest and charge Gomes for the murder of Maria Alves, for which crime he is subsequently convicted.

The only factor that *O Táxi no.9297* really shares with the real-life murder of Maria Alves is the number of the cab, which is the same as the vehicle in which Augusto Gomes killed Alves. The narrative begins with a frame tale. After a fantastic description of New York, which Ferreira had never visited, the narrator describes a club off Broadway. A group of American military officers are dining and conversation turns to a colleague, Lieutenant Francis Hair, who has not been seen for a while. His former superior, Colonel Crowther, informs the diners that Hair is now the American military attaché in Lisbon and 'doing a novel'. One of his colleagues scoffs, reminding his peers that Hair had been a novelist before joining the army. To this aside, Crowther then replies 'I expressed myself badly. When I said that Hair was doing a novel, I did not mean that he was writing one, I meant that he was living one.'[12] Crowther has been receiving letters from Hair relating Hair's adventures, which he volunteers to read aloud to those assembled. In theory, therefore, *O Táxi no.9297* has an epistolary form like *O Mistério* and makes an appeal to some sort of link with actuality as a narrative justification.

The first letter introduces us to Hair. Here it must be said that in form, while *O Táxi no.9297* is divided up into letters, the narrative has nothing in common with the literary features associated with missives (no dates, greetings, sign-offs or asides to a projected correspondent). Instead *O Táxi no.9297* is recounted in a conventional limited first-person narration in which the time of narration coincides with fictional time. The narrative begins with Hair's being in a taxi with an acquaintance, Arsénio de Castro, who realizes that the taxi transporting them is no. 9297, the vehicle in which a young actress named Raquel de Monteverde has been strangled to death. Her killer is still on the loose.

Hair and Castro are on their way to the house of Horácio Vilar, a rich and decadent bohemian. There they meet a group of guests who were invited to spend the weekend. Amongst the group of dissolute characters are two seemingly decent figures, the vulnerable daughter of the murdered actress, Eva, and the generous-spirited Félix do Amaral. It soon becomes apparent that someone holds poor Eva in their thrall and that the same person is also connected to the murder of Raquel de Monteverde. It would seem that the scene is set for an English country-house mystery. Various clever incidents occur that spin the mystery out despite the presence of relatively few suspects. In the end, Hair's suspects boil down to Hair's companion, Arsénio de Castro, the host, Horácio Vilar, and an impresario named Guilherme Dias. *O Táxi no.9297* was originally published as a feuilleton, like much of early Portuguese detective fiction, and the necessarily episodic narrative structure remains. Mário Domingues claims that Repórter X wanted to write like a mix of Conan Doyle and Edgar Allen Poe.[13] Hair's character certainly pays lip service to the sort of cool ratiocination associated with Doyle (and Poe's Lupin), but his actions and the narrative itself are suffused with a dissolute decadence, and the odd preternatural moment is much more reminiscent of other stories by Poe, not to mention a focus on physicality more reminiscent of later, American, hard-boiled detective fiction.

At times it seems as if Reinaldo Ferreira is not quite in control of his material, but in the last letter, when the solution (a solution not really deducible by the reader) is revealed, the events are actually cleverly interlinked, though there are some dubious elements and Repórter X occasionally abuses the technique of the improbable coincidence. In the denouement, Eva's tormentor is murdered and we learn that the suspects belonged to a European spy ring that is attempting to infiltrate America. The plot ends with a return to the frame narrative. Hair's former colleagues are lamenting that his letters to Crowther end, necessarily, without their knowing what happens next. At that moment, the club's butler appears and announces Hair's arrival. He is back in America with his new wife, Eva. Crowther exclaims: 'Eis um romance que acaba como eu gosto: um casamento.'[14] Meaning 'here is a romance that ends the way I like it: with a wedding', it is also a pun on the double meaning of romance in Portuguese (novel, and also 'romance' though this is an anglicism).

With its mix of languid decadence, supernatural touches, constant tension and suspense, not to mention subplots featuring extramarital affairs, myriad forms of drug-taking and international espionage, *O Táxi no.9297* is a lurid but exhilarating novel. It is also imbued with a critical message concerning Portugal. In the end, all the Portuguese (and Spanish) characters are corrupt, or at best hopelessly decadent. The main suspects are found to be involved in espionage against America and against democracy. Hair, on the other hand, is rational and upright, a clean-cut American who embodies modern values and virtues. At the novel's close, he extracts Eva from the miasma of exploitation and repression in which she languishes and delivers her to the epitome of modernity sketched out in the introduction. *O Táxi no.9297* thus continues *O Mistério*'s use of the detective fiction model to entertain and critique. This twofold function is a trait that would fade away under the Salazar dictatorship which, as it established itself, began to stifle the critical voice of popular culture through the offices of the board of censors.

At this time, and into the 1930s, Reinaldo Ferreira's influence over contemporary detective fiction was pervasive. Amongst the other most prolific detective writers of the time were Mário Domingues and Gentil Marques, both of whom wrote in the mould of Repórter X (Marques even going so far as to call himself O Repórter Mistério – the Mystery Reporter). Both Domingues and Marques wrote under their own names and a variety of Anglo-Saxon pseudonyms, a trend that would dominate the next period of detective fiction in Portugal. Nonetheless, it is their orthonymous fiction that is most interesting for today's reader. One of Domingues's more interesting works is *O Preto do 'Charleston'* (1930, The 'Charleston' Black); it is interesting not least because its author, a dark mulatto from the island of São Tomé, seemingly based the novel on his experience of being employed as the doorman of the Clube Ritz in Lisbon.

Dick Haskins's O Jantar É Ás Oito

The next age of Portuguese detective writing gathered pace after the Second World War and represents what Orlando Guerra, echoing Howard Haycroft, calls the 'Golden Age' of Portuguese detective fiction.[15] Yet this would not appear to have been a propitious time for such writing. The *Estado Novo* dictatorship was at its height and, with the machinations of the secret police, the board of censors and the beginning of the wars in Africa, it was a time when 'justice' was only a word in Portugal. Unsurprisingly perhaps, given the lack of leeway available to all forms of cultural expression dealing with national issues, this was an age when Portuguese detective fiction writing most slavishly followed models from abroad and concentrated on intricate yet hermetic plots, and when all the major writers wrote under assumed names. Orlando Guerra writes that this was a period when

> the phenomenon of using pseudonyms seems to be necessary amongst Portuguese authors. On the one hand because of the demands of publishing houses for whom, by preference, an Anglo-Saxon name acts as a magnet; on the other, due to the mental complex that dominates our intellectuals and men of letters who write in a genre they deem a minor one.[16]

Undoubtedly there is much truth in this assertion, but one can but wonder whether there would have been any possibility of publishing populist fiction set in Portugal and presenting disturbances in law and order in the climate of the post-war years.

Popular writers of the so-called 'Golden Age' included Dennis Macshade (the excellent pseudonym of Denis Machado), Edgar Caygill and Ross Pynn (both noms de plume of Roussado Pinto). Of all the Portuguese detective fiction authors of this period, Dick Haskins (António Albuquerque Andrade) is the most successful and the most emblematic, for a number of reasons. The first is that Haskins is reputed to be the most international of Portuguese authors. His work has been published in at least two dozen countries, a rare feat which even Nobel prizewinner José Saramago would be hard pressed to surpass. The second is the typicality of his *oeuvre*. Haskins's novels lie at the crossroads of the two main historical genres of detective fiction: the hard boiled and the cozy. If, on the one hand, Haskins (such as Repórter X's investigator, Dick Haskins's detective is eponymous) is always ready to use his fists, dally with femmes fatales or otherwise and makes frequent references to the comfort of having his large pistol nestling comfortably in its holster, he is also called upon to investigate intricate mysteries that require a memory for details and a flair for deduction. This melange, which is also discernible in Repórter X's *O Táxi no.9297*, is typical of Portuguese detective fiction as it draws upon an amalgam of foreign models and is almost always a hybrid mix of different influences and sub-genres.

The hero in the majority of Haskins's works is a detective also called Dick Haskins, a ploy that again may seem intended to indicate some spurious sense of actuality of events and characters. In the introduction to *O Sono da Morte* (A Deathly Slumber), published as part of a reprint of Haskins's novels almost a decade after its initial publication, Haskins wrote a small biography of his detective in order to bring the reader up to speed. It is here that Haskins introduces the Anglo-Portuguese heritage of his detective (whose father is English and whose mother is Portuguese), something that goes unmentioned in the first novels and plays no real part in his characterization or in determining his actions.The author writes: 'legally Haskins is an English citizen [*sic*], but, morally, he acts under the sway of his Latin temperament, which is what really characterizes his way of feeling and facing up to situations'. He goes on to say: 'Haskins possesses none of the qualities that define the Englishman in every sense of the word: for instance he is not excessively diplomatic, he wears neither bowler hat nor black coat, no flashy trousers or umbrella.'[17] The author began writing at a time when Portuguese detective fiction writers felt little desire to write detective fiction with Portuguese characters and Portuguese settings. As Haskins's career wore on, he chafed increasingly at this constraint, as this rewriting of his detective's past story indicates. In this way, Haskins can be said to have paved the way for the renewal of the genre in the 1980s and 1990s and for its return to Portuguese detectives, Portuguese settings and Portuguese crimes.

The Haskins series features recurring characters and references to previous cases to reward loyal readers. In the novel under consideration here, *O Jantar É Ás Oito* (Dinner is at Eight), there are references to *O Fio da Meada* (Interrupted Thoughts) and *A Sétima Sombra* (The Seventh Shadow), from which various characters appear in the present narrative. Yet these recurrences lend to the Haskins novels none of the qualities of the *roman fleuve* that Danielsson associates with modern detective series (and which only appear in Portuguese detective fiction with Francisco José Viegas's Carvalho/Castanheira novels of the 1990s onwards).[18] The recurrence of these characters functions merely to create a familiar universe. There is no character development and no evolution over time. In the first novel, like James Bond (a character he comes to resemble to an extent in the espionage novels), Haskins loses his wife. From then on in, he has an 'eternal fiancée' called Katy Oughton and, symptomatically, his relationship with her remains exactly the same over the course of the novels. Tellingly, Haskins is not a police detective. He is a journalist, a criminologist and reporter, first for *The Times* and then the *London Daily News*. Even when setting a narrative outside Portugal, it would seem that Portuguese detective fiction writers are uncomfortable with using the figure of a policeman as protagonist. During the dictatorship, the Portuguese constabulary was controlled and exploited by the dictatorship, a situation richly depicted in Cardoso Pires's 1982 novel *Balada da Praia dos Cães* (Ballad of Dog's Beach). One of the main themes of the novel, set in 1960 and with a police inspector as its main character, is the corruption of the notion of justice under a regime which itself committed a crime against a whole society. It is only in the 1990s and with the fading of this memory that Portuguese detective fiction really starts to feature police protagonists.

O Jantar É Ás Oito is characteristic of the Haskins series of novels. Like all the other Haskins novels it is a tightly organized entanglement of plots and subplots. The main strand concerns a man named Michael Robertson Haynes, who has made his fortune embezzling money from his first company, a fraud that has also involved the contract killing of an accountant colleague, Harold Marlowe. Haynes has Marlowe killed by an assassin, Bruno Hurst. Hurst is later arrested and sentenced to twenty-five years for another murder. In the middle of the narrative, we learn that Bruno Hurst has been released. He seeks out Haynes and assaults him. We are told that as a result of this attack Haynes has lost his memory. There follows a complicated denouement in which we discover that Hurst has killed someone else, not Marlowe, and he has allowed the accountant to live in exchange for payment. When Hurst is released, he and Marlowe pursue a complicated plan whereby Hurst kills Haynes and Marlowe has extensive plastic surgery in order to take Haynes's place. It was they who were trying to intimidate Haynes's daughter (though why they do not add her to the list of victims is not explained). In the end, Marlowe double-crosses Hurst and then kills him in a set-up intended to look as if Haynes has reacted in self-defence.

This plot, of which only the general lines are sketched out here, is typical of the intricacy of Haskins's storylines, in which a great many seemingly incidental details are sown along the course of the narrative and flower in the final explanation. If the reader can keep pace with Haskins, there is the possibility (and associated satisfaction) of pre-emptively deducing the denouement. Nonetheless, despite the complexity of the mystery, Haskins, the detective, employs sarcasm and strong-arm tactics as his main weapons. When ratiocination will not provide him with the key to the mystery, Dick Haskins is not averse to forcing the lock. On various occasions he takes a beating and on others he metes one out.

The whole of the narrative is action oriented, told in the first person, with a coincidence of narrative and fictional time. There is neither psychological depiction nor any real concern for sociological and historical matters, except in a very limited way as part of the puzzle. The London in which Haskins lives and investigates is typical of the sort of city used in this type of Portuguese detective fiction: flimsy, stage-set-like and strangely unreal, which, bearing in mind Haskins's idea of the true Englishman, should come as no surprise. For example, even though Haskins is a journalist, he has a butler called Edward. In Haskins's fiction, London in the 1960s is a town in which anyone worth his salt has a manservant.

Generally, however, the details that Haskins uses in *O Jantar É Às Oito* are accurate, even down to street names, although at one point there is mention of someone's opening a pharmacist. There is a level at which the unreal city that Haskins creates is comic, and another level at which it comes to be interesting. The London conjured up in the Haskins novels seems to be a pastiche drawn from a thousand paperbacks and television programmes. It is a city that incorporates already textualized signs and makes little real attempt to give the impression of referring back to a real urban space of concrete, tarmac and movement. Indeed, in *O Jantar É Às Oito* there are various references to what can be inferred to be the inspiration behind the London it pieces together, references to the Hercule Poirot novels and television series such as *The Saint* and *The Avengers*. Indeed, one could say that the Haskins series features the same sort of anachronism as the adventures of John Steed and Emma Peel in *The Avengers*.

O Jantar É Ás Oito is supposed to be set in the present day of its publication, but there is almost no suggestion of the feel, events or ebullience of the 1960s (though the hallucinatory subplot could be read as a sign of the times). The only explicit, if desultory, reference to the times is the inclusion of the minor character of a hippy, whose hirsute appearance prompts the narrator to opine that this member of the flower-power generation looked like 'a fertile terrain for the development of parasites'.[19] It is an observation that speaks volumes about the attitudes and generation of Haskins (as narrative voice and avatar of his creator). Portuguese detective fiction of this period, unlike that which preceded it and that which followed, was artistically conservative and largely cut off from reality.

It may perhaps seem unfair to criticize Dick Haskins for the artificiality of his setting in a work that has no ambition beyond being a cleverly constructed entertainment, especially when any engagement with his surroundings could have led to the book's immediate censorship. A contemporaneous book by Ross Pynn, in which a character showed a marked distaste for war, was banned from circulation, for being counterproductive at a time when the country found itself locked in armed conflict in the colonies (1961–74) and these works had a large readership amongst the conscript soldiers. As well as having a public that perhaps preferred the Anglo-American-style novel, Portugal was a country that, due to censorship, could not be represented in a genre such as the detective novel that demands a degree of realism. More so than reader preference, this probably explains why Portuguese novelists of the period chose to set their works in London, Paris or New York, the capitals of countries where, although justice was imperfect, the words still had meaning and where crime could safely be depicted without attracting the attention of a board of censors.[20] Nonetheless, in Haskins's novels, there is a gradual infiltration of Portuguese themes and settings, giving an indication of the direction that future Portuguese detective fiction would take. This future, however, would have to wait for the dictatorship to end in order to begin.

The first three winners of the Prémio Caminho do Romance Policial:
O Trabalho É Sagrado *(1985),* Perfeito Como Nos Filmes *(1987) and*
Matar a Imagem *(1989)*

After the so-called golden age, the upheaval of the revolution and the decolonization of the Portuguese overseas possessions (which had previously been one of the biggest markets for Portuguese detective fiction), the detective-fiction genre did not really return to the Portuguese literary scene until the 1980s. An important development in that decade was the inauguration of the Prémio Caminho do Romance Policial, a prize first awarded in 1985 and then awarded biannually until 1999. The stage for novels of this genre had been set by several high literary works such as *O Que Diz Molero* (1977, What Molero Says) by Dinis Machado (otherwise known as Dennis Macshade), Mário Zambujal's *Crónica dos Bons Malandros* (1980, Chronicle of the Good Scoundrels), Fernando Namora's *O Rio Triste* (1982, The Sad River) and José Cardoso Pires's *A Balada da Praia dos Cães* (1982, Ballad of Dog's Beach), all of which made use of aspects of, or parodied the detective/crime novel in order to examine the state of the nation, and all of which turned colloquial Portuguese into a literary language.[21] Another 1985 publication was Clara Pinto Correia's *Adeus, Princesa* (Farewell Princess), in which a journalist from Lisbon travels to the Alentejo to investigate the murder of a German NATO soldier, and in the process discovers the social situation of one of Portugal's poorest regions.[22] In the wake of these works, Caminho began a collection integrating new Portuguese detective novels into an anthology comprising the best of foreign detective fiction, and the Prémio Caminho de Literatura Policial gave an immense boost to the genre in Portugal. Though the quality of the home-grown works did not always match that of the foreign imports, the visibility of the prize and the way it placed national detective fiction shoulder to shoulder with the best of its kind written abroad seemed to give a new vigour to the Portuguese scene, and to kick-start home-grown production in the genre. Here I will look at the first three winners, Henrique Nicolau's *O Trabalho É Sagrado* (1985, Work is Sacred), Justino Pamplona and Luis Rodrigues's *Perfeito Como Nos Filmes* (1987, Perfect Like in the Movies) and Ana Teresa Pereira's *Matar a Imagem* (1989, Kill the Image). Together these three works are representative of the sort of Portuguese detective novels published by Caminho, and the way they follow on from the works already discussed and opened up new avenues for the detective fiction genre in Portugal in the 1990s.

Henrique Nicolau is one of the most prolific detective fiction authors of the late 1980s and early 1990s, with novels such as *Alcança Quem Não Cansa* (1987, Finders Keepers), *A Arca do Crime* (1988, The Chest of Crime), *Todos e Nenhum* (1991, All and None) and *Autópsia de um Desatino* (1992, Autopsy of a Folly). Nicolau's *O Trabalho É Sagrado* has, as its principal investigating character, a journalist who remains unnamed (a true Repórter X) thus indicating that the habits of the previous generation are hard to discard. The narrative begins when the journalist protagonist is sent from Lisbon to Oporto to report on a suicide case that seems to be creating problems. The dead man's brother claims that the suicide is in fact a murder, and is not being investigated properly by the police. The journalist's job then is not only to investigate the death of the man, but also to police the police force and look into the suspicious actions of the judiciary. *O Trabalho É Sagrado* is typical of the Caminho detective novels in that it is told in the first person, making extensive use of urban Portuguese slang. There are many weaknesses, however. The plot is loose and the ramifications of the events described are often not followed up. In contrast to the literary use of the detective fiction mould, *O Trabalho É Sagrado* is a full-blown genre novel, and has the weakness of its more mediocre representatives: an excessive concentration on sex and violence, although this is within a libertine rather than misogynistic frame and the investigator displays distaste and contrition for his unduly aggressive acts.

The looseness of the plot means that there is not much of a mystery to *O Trabalho É Sagrado*, although the truth of the investigation remains opaque, representing perhaps the murkiness of the people involved in the crime. As the inquiry advances through hard work and perspiration as opposed to inspiration and intuition, it follows that the novel is deeply rooted in everyday Portuguese urban space. The novel is as much ethnographic description as action, depicting places, foods and drinks, including multiple references to Portuguese life, from politics to football, and constituting a record of the way people spoke in this period. *O Trabalho É Sagrado* has a political angle in that the victim has been involved with smuggling arms to right-wing militia in the aftermath of the revolution and the investigator's enquiry reveals a country in which corruption and collusion between politicians and criminals is rife. The novel ends with the journalist's girlfriend being killed by hit men who are out to murder him and the refusal of the newspaper for which he works to print his report. We leave the investigator as he begins to write up the case in the form of the novel the reader is about to finish.

Justino Pamplona and Luis Rodrigues's *Perfeito Como Nos Filmes* is a much more impressive work, though its plot contains many similarities to its predecessor on the honours list and its authors have not since published any more novels. The principal investigator is a solicitor and private investigator. One of the reasons why journalist protagonists have often been favoured in Portugal is revealed when Henrique Vaz, the investigator, self-consciously mentions that it is illegal in Portugal for a private investigator to make enquiries into a crime. Nonetheless, Vaz agrees to take on the case of Júlio Reis. Again the official verdict is suicide, but Reis's wife disagrees. Vaz learns that Reis was an engineer with a long history of involvement in ultra-left-wing political parties. In the mould of the more speculative detective fiction that would reach its zenith with Francisco Jose Viegas in the 1990s, Vaz's inquiry probes more into the life of the victim than into his death. Through this investigation, Vaz discovers a Portugal that has moved from revolutionary fervour to complicity with an immoral western capitalism and has become disenchanted with the 1980s betrayal of its 1970s ideals. Like *O Trabalho É Sagrado*, *Perfeito Como Nos Filmes* is derived from the American hard-boiled variant of detective fiction, perhaps influenced by the development of the genre in Spain. The puzzle element in Pamplona and Rodrigues's novel is negligible. There are no minutely worked out clues, rather, the case is tackled with pluck, resolve and integrity. For all his ambiguities, the detective is guided by an indefatigable moral compass, although a melancholy realization that right and wrong are not easily distinguishable is never far from the surface. Portugal in the mid-1980s is shown as politically right of centre and plunged into its own form of Thatcherism, leaving those on the left either to throw in their lot with the enemy or to bemoan impotently the days of yore, 'wearing Ana Salazar [a Portuguese fashion designer] trousers and drinking 200 escudo beers [extremely expensive for the time]'.[23] Vaz discovers that Reis has committed suicide, but that he was going to be killed anyway by an extreme left-wing group to which he had been supplying arms and whose anti-capitalist activities were now limited to holding up banks. Along the way, Vaz is beaten up by the police and threatened with much worse, and the purpose of the investigation remains opaque even at the novel's close.

The Portugal in *Perfeito Como Nos Filmes* is one in which the colonial war between 1961 and 1974 still casts a long shadow (there are also references to events in Mozambique and Goa in *O Trabalho É Sagrado*). The investigator and the victim, as well as several of the witnesses, formerly served in Portuguese Guinea (now Guinea-Bissau), perhaps the scene of the worst fighting in the former colonies. In the same way that past military service in Vietnam has been a staple feature for the characterization of disaffected investigators in America, the experience of conscription and the colonial wars is a recurrent feature of Portuguese detective fiction in the Caminho collection and beyond. Indeed, in the 1989 Prémio Caminho de Literatura Policial, ex-soldier António Silveira was awarded an unofficial prize for runners-up for *Morto em Combate* (Killed in Action), a detective fiction novel set in Angola in the 1960s during the colonial war. In the 1990s, the postcolonial detective novel, such as Viegas's *Lourenço Marques* or the Angolan author Pepetela's humorous Jaime Bunda series, would become one of the more interesting subgroups of the crime genre in Portuguese.

Ana Teresa Pereira's *Matar a Imagem* is a much better novel than either of the other Caminho prizewinners, although it is questionable whether it is, indeed, a work of detective fiction, though it obviously branches from the genre. It is perhaps more accurate to call *Matar a Imagem* a thriller. There is no investigator and there is no crime until the novel's close. There are enigmas, and detective fiction recurs in references and tropes. *Matar a Imagem*, rather than recounting the resolution of a mystery, is more concerned with questions of metaphysics and playing out themes of the double and of the labyrinth. The central character is a woman named Rita, so far unsuccessful as a writer, who is caught between her inner world of fiction and fantasies and her desire, from the internalized demands of society, to succeed in her outward social life: success being marriage and the constitution of a family. She weds David, a former boyfriend, whom she has previously left because of his stolidness and lack of imagination. David, it turns out, has his own inner life, one of madness, paranoia and schizophrenia. Once they are married, David wants to return to his home village, the location of which is not explicitly stated, but is deducible as the island of Madeira (the author's place of origin, depicted in the novel as a place of smothering repression). Throughout the novel, the theme of the double takes centre stage, through apparent doppelgängers but also in the form of an interrogation of binaries such as love and hate, love and jealousy, and rationality versus fantasy. Doubles are shown to be reverse images reflected in facing mirrors, identical in appearance but with the points of reference inverted infinitely.

Matar a Imagem points toward Pereira's later novels, such as *As Personagens* (1990, The Characters), *A Última História* (1991, The

Last Story) and *A Cidade Fantasma* (1993, The Ghost City), which do not take place in Portugal. Instead, the setting, as with so many genre fiction in Portugal, is a loosely defined America, a return in a sense to the trend we see in Repórter X and especially Dick Haskins, the fabrication of a fictional world constructed from signs that refer to other, already textualized signs drawn from the world of literature, cinema and television, rather than some putative external reality. A virtual landscape of cultural references becomes the setting for Pereira's work and pre-existing characters drawn from popular culture become frames of reference for new characters of her own invention.

The Caminho prize continued until 1999, by which juncture detective fiction had once again become well established. Other winners include Modesto Navarro (another of the most prominent and prolific Portuguese detective-fiction writers) with *Condenada à Morte* (1991, She was Condemned to Die), Miguel Miranda's *O Estranho Caso do Cadáver Sorridente* (1997, The Strange Case of the Smiling Corpse) and *Apenas Questão de Método* (1999, Merely a Question of How) written by the Luso-Brazilian Cunha de Leiradella and published in 1999. In 1993 and 1995 the prize appears not to have been awarded.

Francisco José Viegas and As Duas Águas do Mar

During the 1990s, Francisco José Viegas has developed into Portugal's most important writer of detective fiction. To date he has published nine novels in the genre: *Crime em Ponta Delgada* (1989, Crime in Ponta Delgada), *Morte no Estádio* (1991, Death in the Stadium), *As Duas Águas do Mar* (1992, The Two Waters of the Sea), *Um Céu Demasiado Azul* (1995, A Too-Blue Sky), *Um Crime na Exposição* (1998, A Crime at the Exhibition), *Um Crime Capital* (2001, A Capital Crime), *Lourenço Marques* in 2002, *Longe de Manaus* (2005, Far From Manaus) and *A Poeira Que Cai Sobre a Terra* (2006, The Dust which Falls to Earth). His work is a fitting point at which to conclude this review of detective fiction in Portugal. Not only does Viegas's work synthesize many of the main trends to be found in the history of the genre in the country, it also points to several of the directions that it may take in the future. Here I will provide a general discussion of the novels Viegas produced in the 1990s and a more in-depth analysis of perhaps his finest work of this period, *As Duas Águas do Mar*. *Um Crime na Exposição* will not be discussed. This novel, like *Um Crime Capital* and *A Poeira Que Cai Sobre a Terra*, was produced as a tie-in (for Expo '98), and also like these other two works, was originally published in a newspaper (a means of publication that stretches back to the very origins of the genre in Portugal). Whilst *Um Crime na Exposição* does deal with the themes and concerns of the earlier novels, it adds relatively little that is new.

Crime em Ponta Delgada, *Morte no Estádio*, *As Duas Águas do Mar* and *Um Céu Demasiado Azul* all concern investigations into murders and their surrounding circumstances which represent a microcosm of the deep shifts in Portuguese society following the end of the *Estado Novo* and the entry of Portugal into the European Union. Each novel is set roughly contemporaneously to the year in which it was published. The post-revolutionary period was a time in which the general patterns of production, consumption and social conditions that held sway in the more developed parts of Europe began to make increasing inroads into a country partially shielded from the wider world by the dictatorship. In short, a parochially rural, religiously observant and socially conservative society suddenly found an urban capitalist, morally secular culture growing up in its midst. Not only did these developments do violence to the image of Portugal fostered by the previous regime, which dominated the nation's self-image, they also definitively supplanted, indeed, were fostered to supplant, a possible Portugal, the one pictured by the communist master narrative that dominated almost all opposition to the *Estado Novo* throughout its almost fifty years of existence and which was tantalizingly glimpsed in the aftermath of the Carnation Revolution of 1974.

As Duas Águas do Mar is Viegas's third novel and has been translated into French and German, as well as being published in Brazil. It is the longest of the novels the author published in the 1990s and is the one in which the major themes of his work in this period are most deeply explored. The novel traces the investigations into the murder of Rui Pedro Martim da Luz in Finisterra, a small town on the Galician coast, and the seemingly accidental drowning of Rita Calado Gomes in the Azores. The detectives begin their investigations individually, but the two cases soon merge when it is discovered that Luz and Gomes were once lovers. Over the course of the investigation, a detailed biography of Luz is pieced together. Formerly an idealistic student with communist sympathies who, after 'fifty years of grubbing money by almost any means possible' including minor industrial espionage for the Portuguese secret service, had tried to leave this existence behind and start afresh.[24] He quits his job as a high-powered lawyer and moves to Finisterra, to write, marry a local girl and open a hotel in partnership with a local man with whom he may or may not have been having a sexual relationship. Rather than any figure from his controversial past, we discover that it was the local girl and Luz's partner who murdered him, upon discovering that Luz planned to forsake his life in Finisterra and effect a reconciliation with Gomes, a former partner. Filipe Castanheira, the other detective featured in the series, then discovers that Gomes has not died accidentally. In fact, she has been the victim of a meticulously planned and ruthlessly executed murder. The killer was her best friend, also a former partner of Luz's, who was insanely jealous at the prospect that Gomes might achieve the happiness she was unable to secure.

Luz's life is another of the broken lives that Viegas's detectives recurrently discover in the course of their investigations, existences that have somehow failed or gone awry. Murder, for Luz as for the other victims in the series, comes at the point when the contradiction between life as it was dreamt of in the past and life as it wears on in the present becomes untenable. In 1990s novels, life as it was projected in the past is often, as in the case of Luz, an idealistically communist one. This ideological leaning, the reader learns, was also an intrinsic part of the youth of both detectives, and it is an understanding of how their lives do not match up either to the ideals of their youth that allows the two investigators the sort of empathy needed to understand and eventually close their cases. For Kirsten Ross, detective fiction has the tendency to 'take as one of its principal tasks the representation of the ordinary, everyday entanglement of people with their surroundings'.[25] In *As Duas Águas do Mar*, we see the detectives struggling with the surroundings in which the victims also lived, against the backdrop of a mutual past, revealing the tenor of modern life in Portugal, and in doing so discovering the reasons behind their murder.

In place of the bright tomorrows promised in their youths, the victims in the 1990s are often embroiled in strings of sexual affairs or shady financial dealings, which serve only to create the illusion of satisfaction and power. As policemen, Ramos and Castanheira have little connection with the high-powered worlds in which the victims often move, but they are shown to be subject to similar pressures within their own private lives. Both Ramos and Castanheira struggle in second marriages fraught with problems. For the murderer, the victim and the detectives alike, the Catholic ideal of the lifelong marriage has broken down irretrievably. Again, it is the empathy felt by the investigators, often towards all parties involved in the case, which proves to be the key to solving the crime. Frequently, as in *As Duas Águas do Mar*, it is those who have been wronged in the victim's attempt to recover the dreams of youth who commit the murder, thus lending a downbeat and tragic air to much of the series. As George Grella has observed of the hard-boiled novel, for Ramos and Castanheira the successful investigation becomes a type of defeat through its revelations, often concerning a man of their generation, with similar hopes and aspirations and, ultimately, not dissimilar failings.[26]

The generally pessimistic mood that permeates the Viegas novels of the 1990s is counteracted by two facts: the friendship between the two detectives and the way in which they manage to find compensation in their shared pleasure in food, often within the space of this friendship, which acts as a sort of island away from the demands of their enquiries and the pressures of their everyday lives. This simple pleasure, for the investigators, functions as an antidote to the poisons of the world that surrounds them, much as they do for Vázquez Montalbán's Pepe Carvalho. In a world accelerating into late capitalism and undergoing a breakneck, reckless mutation of values, the degradation of eating habits demonstrates a clearly diagnosable symptom of what has gone wrong, and is a trait, unlike the general conditions with which the detectives struggle, that can be clearly and uncomplicatedly remedied within the detectives' own lives. Both Ramos and Castanheira come from northern Portugal, and both cook the food they remember from their childhood – maintaining their connections to their families, their homes, their roots and their memories – or dishes created with ingredients that are pure and good, in stark contrast to the murky world that envelopes them in their professional lives. It is no accident that Ramos and Castanheira concentrate as much on the preparation as on the consumption of their food. It is a creative transformation of the world, one that stands in stark contrast to the economic and social transformations being wrought in Portuguese society at that time.

The novels in these five cases represent the general lines of development in detective fiction on the Portuguese literary scene and pave the way for the current state of the genre in the nation today. The detective fiction model continues to hold a fascination for some of Portugal's most respected contemporary novelists, and can be discerned in works such as António Lobo Antunes's latest novel *O Meu Nome É Legião* (2007, My Name is Legion), which, alternating between police reports and the experiences of a teenage gang, tackles themes of crime, violence and delinquency on Lisbon's multi-ethnic periphery, and Lídia Jorge's *Combateremos a Sombra* (2007, We Shall Fight the Shade*)*, in which a psychoanalyst attempts to decipher a message brought to her by an ex-patient and becomes entangled in a web of personal and political deception.

On a more popular note, new authors in the genre have made their appearance. Rui Araújo, a journalist with state television company Rádio Televisão Portuguesa, has published *À Queima-Roupa* (2000, Point Blank), *Lisbon Killer* (2004) and *A Amante Fatal* (2005, The Deadly Lover). *Lisbon Killer*, perhaps his most interesting work, follows the hunt for a serial killer whose crimes are terrorizing society on the outskirts of Lisbon. The two investigating officers are Miguel Neves and António Nicolau of the Polícia Judiciária. The narrative incorporates elements drawn from a true crime story and is related in the terse, blunt language of those fighting crime on the streets of Lisbon – the author spent months accompanying the Portuguese police in preparation – and has a metafictional dimension, in so far as the plot also features a journalist writing a report on serial killers. *Lisbon Killer* goes beyond the lurid style of Repórter X to approach the police procedural and give an intimation of what real-life crime fighting entails. On a slightly less realistic note is another newly emerged writer of detective fiction, Miguel Ávila, who, with *Fraude na City* (2004, Fraud in the City), brings us Michael Castro, a young Londoner of Portuguese descent, who finds himself embroiled in a case of corruption in the City. Alternating action, suspense and a description of today's London, including the areas inhabited by the Portuguese diaspora, it is both contemporary yet also somehow redolent of the golden age of crime fiction, in a way that recollects the work of Dick Haskins. Ávila, who lives and works in London, also published *A Tentação de Dinheiro* (The Temptation of Money) in 2004, set around similar themes. In both authors elements of previous trends in Portuguese crime fiction can be found, but these are realized in much more convincing ways. *Lisbon Killer* marries fact and fiction in an entirely convincing and completely entertaining way, whereas *Fraude na City* creates a plausible Luso-English character who inhabits a city that, while not disconnected from actuality, is still the London of a thousand detective novels.

The major figure in Portuguese detective fiction in the 2000s remains Francisco José Viegas. After *Lourenço Marques* in 2002, Viegas published *Longe de Manaus* in 2005. Perhaps his finest work to date, it was awarded the Grande Prémio de Romance e Novela prize by the Associação Portuguesa de Escritores, a first for detective fiction in the country. The novel centres on the investigations of Jaime Ramos into the death of a man whose body is found on the outskirts of Oporto. Like the other novels in Viegas's body of work, *Longe de Manaus* is as much an inquiry into biographies – of the victim, of the killer and of the detective – as into the places in which their existences have unfolded: Ramos's home of Oporto; Manaus, the capital of the Brazilian state of Amazónia; nineteenth-century Beirut, from where many Lebanese emigrated to Brazil; Angola, where the killer himself fought in the colonial war; and Guinea-Bissau, where Ramos served in the Portuguese army. One of the successful aspects of the novel lies in the way in which the language in which it is narrated shifts from European Portuguese to Brazilian Portuguese, depending on the nationality of the character speaking. In *Longe de Manaus*, Viegas returns to and elaborates on his long-running themes of the painful persistence of ever fragile memory, the painful equivocations of modern life and the midlife melancholy of its protagonist within a framework that criss-crosses the Atlantic, establishing links between contemporary Portuguese fiction and the human and physical geographies of Africa and South America.

The actual state of detective fiction in Portugal seems to be just as it ever was: appearing in fits and starts, yet throwing up interesting work, in genre-based novels with both fanciful and realist tendencies, but often having its techniques then incorporated into more literary fiction. Perhaps in the future a 'sixth case' will break the mould. Only time will tell.

* * *

Extract from *As Duas Águas do Mar* (The Two Waters of the Sea) by Francisco José Viegas

This scene takes place after the murder on a remote beach in Galicia of Rui Pedro Martim da Luz, the first of the two victims. Jaime Ramos has just received official permission to open the case. Before searching the dead man's house and delving into his story, the detective holds forth on the philosophy of life:

The night was wearing on. They had arrived at about half past eight and, for the past four hours, after having asked the concierge for the key and received her grumpy cooperation, they had made a search through three rooms of Rui Pedro Martim da Luz's vast apartment. Jaime Ramos had left the office until last, and had brought the photographs back through to the front room where Isaltino de Jesus was looking over the contents of the wine rack.

The documents had been brought to his office early that afternoon. You can get to work on it now, were the chief inspector's words. Jaime Ramos had smiled and lit a cigar. He then waited for night to fall, consuming the time in silence.

'It'll be easier to work on it now,' said Jaime Ramos to Isaltino de Jesus, who had brought him the blue card folder.

'Easier?'

'Of course. Now we have authorization.'

'If you say so, boss.'

'I need to speak to all these people: father-in-law, brother-in-law, his parents are deceased, the secretaries from his office, concierge, closest friends, like this Ernesto das Neves Oliveira, whom we already know about. Never choose a wife with an unwieldy name, Isaltino, because you'll have to pass it on to your children.'

'My wife's got a normal surname, boss. Machado.'

'You're married?'

'Got married eight years ago.'

'I hadn't noticed. You were young.'

'Twenty-three.'

'You're a fast worker, Isaltino. But careful with the name if you ever have to choose another wife. Machado de Jesus's not bad, it could be worse, that's true enough. It's nothing out of the ordinary. Do you have any children?

'No. Not yet.'

'You should have children, Isaltino. A child is an adventure. Then you don't have to go looking elsewhere, get my drift? You don't have to go cast your eye over other things. A man should just get married once, know one woman, die only once.'

'But you're divorced, boss.'

'But I'm nobody, Isaltino. I'm a bad example. I've failed at everything.'

'Well ... at almost everything. This year FC Porto didn't win the championship, restaurants are going to have smoking areas, and they'll probably knock down the farms that are clinging on by their fingernails behind my neighbourhood, those that face down towards the river.'

'They already have knocked them down, boss.'

'I didn't notice. I don't notice anything, which means I'm getting old. When they get rid of the things you like it means you're getting old. These days there are people that try their hardest to like anything newfangled because that way they dodge old age. Modern singers, for example. And modern writers. And younger football players. And new cars with automatic transmission. They keep the age they had when they first started to learn how to like new things.'

'Don't you like the new young footballers, boss?'

'No.'

'Not even the new young FC Porto players?'

'Not even the new young FC Porto players. I wouldn't even like myself if I were new and young. A man, Isaltino, should learn to grow old and realize that his time has passed. If we grow old graciously, it's because we're happy, or we were happy when we began to grow old. It's a great art. The only thing that's worth being really good at. That's why I like these cigars. Look here, Isaltino. They're an old brand that doesn't appear on television commercials or in the magazines that your wife reads. Have you ever smoked a cigar like this one?'

'No. Cigars are too strong.'

'No they're not. That's the way they're meant to be. You say they're strong because you're comparing them to the cigarettes you smoke, but cigars have always been like this. They only make one of these cigars every twenty minutes; in the whole world there is only one place where they make these cigars, on an island on the other side of the world, on this world at least.'

'All the same they are strong, boss' said Isaltino de Jesus, putting down the folder at last, and taking a seat. 'We can go to the apartment tomorrow morning, I've already informed the family, and it's always as well to inform the family when you've got to look over the victim's belongings. I said we'd be there at ten. Ten, half past ten. The concierge has the key.'

'We're going tonight, Isaltino, in a little while, before dinner even, if we can.

I've waited a week for this authorization to come through, I'm not going to let it get cold now.'

'That might not go down well.'

'No, maybe not, but that's their problem. We'll get to the house around eight. Go and eat something. That way, we'll be able to take our time looking around, as much time as we like, and we don't give them a chance to tidy up or hide anything, if they haven't already.'

They hadn't. Jaime Ramos, unaccustomedly, was able to rummage around as much as he liked, until he found the pile of photographs from Finisterra, so absolutely banal, so ordinary. A tumbledown wall, the balcony of a house, supposedly that of Rui Pedro Martim da Luz's house in Finisterra. In another photograph a woman is laughing. In photographs everyone is always smiling. She is a small woman, her light-coloured eyes peep through her straight hair, her neck is slender, her hand is stretched out towards the lens, as if to say 'don't take pictures of me', Jaime Ramos thinks.

'Isaltino.'

'Boss.'

'This man was a fool. With fools you always have to be careful, because they trick us more easily, even though we're smarter than they are. Smarter in everything: we're not vain, we hide almost nothing, we're

simple people and we have no money. This man was a fool with a lot of money, tons of it, he could trick us all the more easily.'
He put the photographs away in their box.
'But we've got his number, haven't we?'
'If you say so, boss,' said Isaltino de Jesus in agreement, sorting through another pile of books.

Francisco José Viegas, *As Duas Águas do Mar* (Oporto: Asa, 1992), pp. 253–7. Translated by Paul M. Castro.

Notes

[1] See Orlando Guerra, 'A literatura policial Portuguesa e os escritores marginais', *Vertice: Revista de Cultura e Arte*, 45 (December 1991), 101–5; Ana Isabel Briones, 'Género e contragénero: tópicos do romance policial na narrativa Portuguesa como via de reflexão Histórica', *Revista de Filologia Românica*, 15, (1998), 267–80; and Mafalda Ferin Cunha, 'A tentação do romance policial no romance Português contemporâneo', *Colóquio Letras*, 161/162 (July 2002), 275–94.

[2] See Briones, 'Género e contragénero', 267–80. Briones's excellent analysis considers Fernando Namora's *O Rio Triste*, Nuno Bragança's *Square Tolstoi* and Clara Pinto Correia's *Adeus, Princesa*, yet only the latter is deemed to have any real connection to the detective-fiction genre.

[3] Guerra, 'A literatura policial Portuguesa e os escritores marginais', 100.

[4] Ibid., 101.

[5] Ernesto Guerra da Cal, *Lengua y estilo de Eça de Queiroz* (Coimbra: University Press, 1975).

[6] Ofélia Paiva Monteiro, 'Um jogo humorítico com a verosimilhança romanesca: *O Mistério da Estrada de Sintra*', *Colóquio Letras*, 86 (July 1985), 16–17.

[7] Ibid., 17.

[8] Guerra, 'A literatura policial Portuguesa', 102.

[9] See José Lança-Coelho, 'Pessoa e o romance policial', *Vertice: Revista de Cultura e Arte*, 45 (December 1991), 117–19, for a discussion of Pessoa's dabblings with detective fiction.

[10] In Reinaldo Ferreira, *O Táxi no.9297* [Taxi 9297] (Lisbon: Círculo de Leitores, 1986), p. 17.

[11] See Pedro Rosa, *Reinaldo Ferreira 1897–1935* (Lisbon: Camara Municipal de Lisboa, 1998), for details.

[12] Ferreira, *O Táxi no.9297*, p. 3, my translation.

[13] Rosa, *Reinaldo Ferreira 1897–1935*.

[14] Ferreira, *O Táxi no.9297*, p. 323.

[15] Guerra, 'A literatura policial Portuguesa', 102.

[16] Ibid., my translation.

[17] Dick Haskins, *O Jantar É Ás Oito* [Dinner is at Eight] (Lisbon: Dêagá, 1973).
[18] See Karin Molander, *The Model Detective: Special Interest and Seriality in Contemporary Detective Fiction* (Uppsala: Uppsala University, 2002).
[19] Haskins, *O Jantar É Ás Oito*, p. 184, my translation.
[20] A fascinating question to consider is what sort of detective fiction set in Portugal would have passed the censors.
[21] See Briones, 'Género e contragénero', for *O Rio Triste*, and Briones, 'Género e contragénero', Helena Kaufman, 'A sociedade portuguesa sob investigação em *Balada da Praia dos Cães* by José Cardoso Pires and *Adeus, Princes*', *Hispania*, 62, 4 (1993), 644–71, and Melo e Castro, 'José Cardoso Pires's *Balada de Praia dos Cães*', for *Balada da Praia dos Cães*.
[22] See Kaufman, 'A sociedade portuguesa', for a more in-depth discussion
[23] Justino Pamplona and Luís Rodrigues, *Perfeito Como Nos Filmes* [Perfect Like in the Movies] (Lisbon: Caminho, 1987), p. 34, my translation.
[24] Francisco José Viegas, *As Duas Águas do Mar* [The Two Waters of the Sea] (Oporto: Asa, 1992), p. 50, my translation.
[25] Kirsten Ross, 'Watching the detectives', in F. Barker, P. Hulme and M. Iversen (eds), *Postmodernism and the Re-reading of Modernity* (Manchester: Manchester University Press, 1992), p. 68.
[26] George Grella, 'The hard-boiled detective novel', in Robin W. Winks (ed.), *Detective Fiction: A Collection of Critical Essays* (Englewood Cliffs: Prentice, 1980), pp. 109–10.

Bibliography

Araújo, Rui, *À Queima-Roupa* [Point Blank] (Lisbon: Terramar, 2000).
——, *Lisbon Killer* (Lisbon: Oficina do Livro, 2004).
——, *A Amante Fatal* [The Deadly Lover] (Lisbon: Oficina do Livro, 2005).
Ávila, Miguel, *A Tentação do Dinheiro* [The Temptation of Money] (Barcarena: Presença, 2004).
——, *Fraude na City* [Fraud in the City] (Barcarena: Presença, 2004).
Briones, Ana Isabel, 'Género e contragénero: tópicos do romance policial na narrativa Portuguesa como via de reflexão Histórica', *Revista de Filologia Românica*, 15, (1998), 267–80.
Cardoso Pires, José, *A Balada da Praia dos Cães* [Ballad of Dog's Beach] (Lisbon: O Jornal, 1982).
Chagas, João, *O Crime da Sociedade: Romance de Palpitante Actualidade* (Lisbon: Libanio e Cunha, 1897).
Correia, Clara Pinto, *Adeus, Princesa* [Farewell Princess] (Lisbon: Relógio d'Água, 1985).
Costa, Luís Filipe, *Agora e na Hora da Sua Morte* (Lisbon: Caminho, 1988).
Cunha, Mafalda Ferin, 'A tentação do romance policial no romance Português contemporário', *Colóquio Letras*, 161/162 (July 2002), 275–94.

Domingues, Mário, *O Preto do 'Charleston'* [The 'Charleston' Black] (Lisbon: Guimaraes, 1930).
Ferreira, Reinaldo, *O Mistério da Rua Saraiva de Carvalho* (Lisboa: Guimarães Editores, 1919).
——, *Preto e Branco* [Black and White] (Lisbon: Barata-Martins, 1923).
——, *A Virgem do Bristol Club* [The Bristol Club Virgin] (Oporto: Primeiro de Janeiro, 1930).
——, *O Táxi no.9297* [Taxi 9297] (1926; reprint Lisboa: Círculo de Leitores, 1986).
Fialho de Almeida, José Valentim, *O Roubo* (reprint Lisboa: Typografia Universal, 1882).
Grella, George, 'The hard-boiled detective novel', in Robin W. Winks (ed.), *Detective Fiction: A Collection of Critical Essays* (Englewood Cliffs: Prentice, 1980), pp. 103–20.
Guerra, Orlando, 'A literatura policial Portuguesa e os escritores marginais', *Vertice: Revista de Cultura e Arte*, 45 (December 1991), 101–5.
Guerra da Cal, Ernesto, *Lengua y estilo de Eça de Queiroz* (Coimbra: University Press, 1975).
Haskins, Dick, *O Fio da Meada* [Interrupted Thoughts] (Lisbon: Livraria Ática, 1960).
——, *O Sono da Morte* [A Deathly Slumber] (Lisbon: Dêagá, 1972).
——, *O Jantar É Ás Oito* [Dinner is at Eight] (Lisbon: Dêagá, 1973).
——, *A Sétima Sombra* [The Seventh Shadow] (Lisbon: Dêagá, 1974).
Jorge, Lídia, *Combateremos a Sombra* [We Shall Fight the Shade] (Lisbon: Dom Quixote, 2007).
Kaufman, Helena, 'A sociedade portuguesa sob investigação em *Balada da Praia dos Cães* by José Cardoso Pires and *Adeus, Princes*', *Hispania*, 62, 4 (1993), 644–71.
Lança-Coelho, José, 'Pessoa e o romance policial', *Vertice: Revista de Cultura e Arte*, 45 (December 1991), 117–19.
Leiradella, Cunha de, *Apenas Questão de Metódo* [Merely a Question of How] (Lisbon: Caminho, 1999).
Leite Bastos, Francisco, *Os Crimes de Diogo Alves* (Lisbon: Liv. Ed. de Matos Moreira, 1877).
——, *As Tragedias de Lisboa*, vols 1–4 (Lisbon: Typographia das Horas Romanticas, 1878–9).
Lobo Antunes, António, *O Meu Nome É Legião* [My Name is Legion] (Lisbon: Dom Quixote, 2007).
Machado, Dinis, *O Que Diz Molero* [What Molero Says] (Amadora: Bertrand, 1977).
Melo e Castro, Paul, 'José Cardoso Pires's *Balada de Praia dos Cães*: historiographic metafiction and the detective novel', *Romance Studies*, 28, 2 (2010), 130–40.
Miranda, Miguel, *O Estranho Case do Cadáver Sorridente* [The Strange Case of the Smiling Corpse] (Lisbon: Caminho, 1998).
Molander, Karin, *The Model Detective: Special Interest and Seriality in Contemporary Detective Fiction* (Uppsala: Uppsala University, 2002).

Namora, Fernando, *O Rio Triste* [The Sad River] (1870; reprint Lisbon: Círculo de Leitores, 1983).
Navarro, Modesto, *Condenada à Morte* [She was Condemned to Die] (Lisbon: Caminho, 1991).
Nicolau, Henrique, *O Trabalho É Sagrado* [Work is Sacred] (Lisbon: Caminho, 1985).
——, *Alcança Quem Não Cansa* [Finders Keepers] (Lisbon: Caminho, 1987).
——, *A Arca do Crime* [The Ghost of Crime] (Lisbon: Caminho, 1988).
——, *Todos e Nenhum* [All and None] (Lisbon: Caminho, 1991).
——, *Autópsia de um Desatino* [Autopsy of a Folly] (Lisbon: Caminho, 1992).
Paiva Monteiro, Ofélia, 'Um jogo humorístico com a verosimilhança romanesca: *O Mistério da Estrada de Cintra*', *Colóquio Letras*, 86 (July 1985), 15–23.
Pamplona, Justino and Luis Rodrigues, *Perfeito Como Nos Filmes* [Perfect Like in the Movies] (Lisbon: Caminho, 1987).
Pepetela, *Jaime Bunda: Agente Secreto* (Lisbon: Dom Quixote, 2001).
Pereira, Ana Teresa, *Matar a Imagem* [Kill the Image] (Lisbon: Caminho, 1989).
——, *As Personagens* [The Characters] (Lisbon: Editorial Caminho, 1990).
——, *A Última História* [The Last Story] (Lisbon: Caminho, 1991).
——, *A Cidade Fantasma* [The Ghost City] (Lisbon: Caminho, 1993).
Queiroz, Eça de and Ramalho Ortigão, *O Misterio da Estrada de Sintra* [The Sintra Road Mystery] (Lisbon: Círculo de Leitores, 1983).
Rosa, Pedro, *Reinaldo Ferreira 1897–1935* (Lisbon: Camara Municipal de Lisboa, 1998).
Ross, Kristin, 'Watching the detectives', in F. Barker, P. Hulme and M. Iversen (eds), *Postmodernism and the Re-reading of Modernity* (Manchester: Manchester University Press, 1992), pp. 57–77.
Silveira, António, *Morto em Combate* [Killed in Action] (Lisbon: Caminho, 1990).
Viegas, Francisco José, *Crime em Ponta Delgada* [Crime in Ponta Delgada] (Mem Martins: Europa-América, 1989).
——, *Morte no Estádio* [Death in the Stadium] (Lisbon: Círculo de Leitores, 1991).
——, *As Duas Águas do Mar* [The Two Waters of the Sea] (Oporto: Asa, 1992).
——, *Um Céu Demasiado Azul* [A Too Blue Sky] (Oporto: Asa, 1995).
——, *Um Crime na Exposição* [A Crime at the Exhibition] (Oporto: Asa, 1998).
——, *Lourenço Marques* (Oporto: Asa, 2002).
——, *Longe de Manaus* [Far from Manaus] (Oporto: Asa, 2005).
——, *Um Crime Capital* [A Capital Crime] (Oporto: Asa, 2000).
——, *A Poeira Que Cai Sobre a Terra* [The Dust which Falls to Earth] (Vila Nova de Familicão: Visão, 2006).
Zambujal, Mário, *Crónica dos Bons Malandros* [Chronicle of the Good Scoundrels] (Amadora: Bertrand, 1980).

Index

Alarcón, Pedro Antonio de 1
   clavo, El 1
Alarcos Llorach, E. 12
Alianza Popular 48 n.
Alvarez, Blanca 85
   niñas no hacen ruido cuando mueren, Las 85
   soledad del monstruo, La 85
Anderson, Benedict 52
Aranda, Vicente 24 n.
Arcos, Lais 85
   72 horas 85
Aritzeta, Margarida 57, 87–8
   cau del llop, El 87–8
Asensi, Matilde 87–8
   salón de ámbar, El 87–8
Atxaga, Bernardo 51, 64–8
   Gizona bere bakardadean (*Un hombre solo*) 51, 65, 67–71
Auden, W. H. 6, 8
   'Guilty Vicarage, The' 6
autonomous regions 3, 55
Aznar, José María 14

Ballesteros Gaibrois, Mercedes (pseud. Rocq Morris) 76
   City Hotel 76
   París-Niza 76
Balzac, Honoré 12
Basque Country
   failed community 51
Bazán, Emilia Pardo 1–2, 75–6
   gota de sangre, La 1, 75
Benet, Juan 14
   Aire de un crimen, El 14
Brigada Criminal 16, 96

Cain, James M. 10
Cantar del Mío Cid 1

Capmany, Maria-Aurèlia 56, 76
   jaqué de la democracia, El 76
Careta i Vidal, Antoni 9
Carvalho, Pepe 13, 28–9, 32–5, 38–47
Castro, Mercedes 86
   Y punto 86
Catalonia 3, 9, 34, 46, 51, 53–5, 57–60, 68, 78, 80, 85
Chandler, Raymond 3, 8–9, 32, 79
Christie, Agatha 6, 10, 76
Círculo de Crimen 15
Civil Guard, Spanish 58–9
civil war *see* Spanish Civil War
Clau de vidre radio series 79
Colmeiro, José 12, 14, 38, 75, 98–9
Conan Doyle, Arthur 10, 56, 75, 78, 122
   Study in Scarlet, A 1, 78
Craig-Odders, Renée W. 15, 19, 24 n.
crime fiction
   Basque 3, 17–18, 51–73
   Catalan 2, 9–11, 15–18, 20, 22 n., 30, 35, 41, 44, 51–73, 76, 78–90
   Galician 51–74: Galician modernity 62; Galician stereotypes 60–7
Cua de Palla 9, 56
'culebrones lésbicos' 84

Dante Alighieri 12
de León, Rafael 13
Delmar, E. C. 2, 21 n.
   misterio del contador, El 2, 21 n.
   tórtola de la puñalada, La 2, 21 n.
   Piojos grises 2, 21 n.
Demasiado para Gálvez 18
División Azul 21 n.
Don Quixote 14, 35

Index

Dostoevsky, Fyodor 6
 Crime and Punishment 6
Duque de Rivas, el 1
 'antigüalla de Sevilla, Una' 1

ETA (Euskadi ta Askatasuna) 17, 20, 65–8, 107–8

Fagés, Marta 85
 Amores prohibidos 85
Fanny Pelopaja 24
FBI 7, 59
Fernando VII 7
First Spanish Republic 19
Franc, Isabel (pseud. Lola Van Guardia) 83–5, 88
 Plumas de doble filo 84
 mansión de las tribadas, La 84–5
 No me llames cariño 85
Franco, Francisco 15, 19, 28, 32, 36, 53–4, 56, 63, 65–6, 75–7, 80–1, 83, 87, 94, 100
Franco regime
 cultural and linguistic policies 54, 76
Fuster, Jaume 11, 41, 51, 57, 79
 De mica en mica, s'omple la pica 11, 57
 Sota el signe de Sagitari 57–8, 68

García Lorca, Federico 19
García Pavón, Francisco 11–13, 20–1, 22 n.
 'De cómo el Quaque mató al hermano Folión y del curioso ardid que tuvo el guardia Plinio para atraparle' 23 n.
 hermanas coloradas, Las 11
 Reinado de Witza 11, 22 n.
 vendimiario de Plinio, El 13, 21

Generation of 98 12
Giménez-Bartlett, Alicia 80–3, 86, 88
 barco cargado de arroz, Un 81, 83
 Día de perros 81, 83
 Mensajeros de la oscuridad 81, 83
 Muertes de papel 81
 Nido vacío 81, 83

 Ritos de muerte 81, 83
 Serpientes en el paraíso 81, 83
 silencio de los claustros, El 81
globalization 43, 76, 104
Godsland, Shelley 76, 82
González Ledesma, Francisco 30, 35, 44, 95–8
 novela de barrio, Una 96
Grau, Anna 87
 día que va morir el president, El 87
Grosso, Alfonso 18, 35
 invitados, Los 18
 Otoño indio 18
Guardia Civil 18–19, 102
Guerra Garrido, Raúl 17, 20
 Lectura insólita de 'El capital' 17, 20

Hammett, Dashiel 3, 9–10, 32
hard-boiled fiction 3–4, 7, 13, 19–20, 29, 32, 34, 36, 39, 57–8, 77–8, 80, 84, 88, 98–9, 106–7, 123, 131
Harper's 6
Hart, Patricia 77, 81
 Spanish Sleuth, The 3
Himes, Chester 9
Holmes, Sherlock 1, 19, 56, 59, 76, 78

Ibáñez, Julián 17
imagined communities 52–6
Imser Siglo 107–8
Inspector Méndez 95
Irons, Glenwood 77

James, P. D. 79
 Unsuitable Job for a Woman, An 79
Jordana, C. A. 9

Kafka, Franz 6, 8
 Trial, The 6, 8
knight errant 12

Lacruz, Mario 3, 8–12
 inocente, El 3, 8–11

146

language
    identity 54–60
    policy 54–5, 59
Law of Historical Memory 87
linguistic clues 58
'lladres i serenos' 9
loco-cuerdo 14

Machado, Antonio 13
    Campos de Castilla 13
Madrid, Juan 16–21, 30, 35, 44, 99
    apariencias no engañan, Las 16, 50
    aventura del tocador de señoras, La 14, 23 n., 97
    beso de amigo, Un 16
    Cuentas pendientes 17
    Días contados 20
    Gente bastante extraña 17
    Grupo de noche 17
    Malos tiempos 17
    Nada que hacer 16
    Regalo de la casa 17, 44
    Restos de carmín 17
    Tánger 17
    trabajo fácil, Un 17
Margenat, Asumpta 87–8
    Escapa't d'Andorra 87–8
Mallorcan fiction 11, 57, 78–9
Mandel, Ernest 7
    Delightful Murder: A Social History of the Crime Story 7
Mar-Molinaro, Claire 17 n.
Maresma, Assumpta 87
    complot dels anells, El 87
Marlowe, Philip 11, 16, 100
Martín, Andreu 11, 15–18, 20, 30, 35, 44, 57
    A la vejez, navajazos 15
    Aprende y calla 15
    No demanis llobarro for a de temporada 16
    Prótesis 15–16, 24, 50
    Si es, no es 16, 44
    Sr. Capone no está en casa, El 15
Martínez Reverte, Jorge 18, 20, 35, 44
    Gálvez en Euskadi 18, 20, 44

Gálvez en la frontera 18
Gálvez y el cambio del Cambio 18
Gudari Gálvez 18, 20
Mendoza, Eduardo 13–14, 23 n., 51, 93, 97–8
    aventura del tocador de señoras, La 14, 23 n., 97
    asombroso viaje de Pomponio Flato, El 97
    ciudad de los prodigios, La 14
    laberinto de las aceitunas, El 14, 97
    misterio de la cripta embrujada, El 13, 97
    verdad sobre el caso Savolta, La 13
'mini-boom' 14–15
Miralles, Alberto 18
    semana pintada de negro, Una 18

novela criminal 10, 47 n.

O'Connor, Patricia 12
Ofèlia Dracs collective 57, 78
    Negra i consentida 78
Oliver, Maria-Antónia 11, 35, 57, 78–90
    Antípodes 79, 94
    Estudi en lila 78, 80, 88–9
    'On ets, Mònica?' 78
    sol que fa l'ànec, El 79
Ortigão, Ramalho 2, 4, 117
    Mistério de Estrada de Sintra 2, 4, 117, 120–1
    see also Queiroz, Eça de
Ortiz, Lourdes 14, 18, 31, 76–80
    Picadura mortal 14, 18, 31, 77

Poal-Aregall, M. 56
Paredes Nuñez, Juan 75
Pedrolo, Manuel de 9–11, 22 n., 56
    Algú que no hi havia de ser 10
    Es vessa una sang fàcil 10
    Joc brut 10–11
    Inspector fa tard, L' 10
    Mossegar-se la cua 10
    Pas de ratlla 10
Piquer, Concha 13

Index

Plinio 11–13, 20–3
PNV (Partido Nacionalista Vasco) 17
Poe, Edgar Allan 1, 7, 10, 100, 119, 122–3
  'Murders in the Rue Morgue' 1, 7
Por amor al arte 16
Porter, Dennis 58
Premio de la Crítica 11, 13
Premio Eugenio Nadal 11
Premio Nacional de las Letras Españolas 17
Premio Nacional de Literatura Infantil y Juvenil 16
Proust, Marcel 12

Queiroz, Eça de 2, 4, 117–19
  Mistério de Estrada de Sintra, O 2, 4, 117, 120–1

Rapto de las sabinas 11
Reagan, Ronald 14, 23
Reig, Rafael 104–5, 109
  Guapa de cara 104–5
  Sangre a borbotones 104–5
Reigosa, Carlos G. 51, 60, 62–3
  Crime en Compostela 51, 60–3, 68
Reinado de Witza 11, 22 n.
Ribas, Rosa 86–7
  Entre dos aguas 86
Ribera, Jaume 16
Ripoll, Cayetano 7
Roberto Esteban 98–9, 110–11
Rodoreda, Mercè 2, 76
  Crim 2, 76
roman noir 8, 16, 98
Ruiz Zafón, Carlos 103–4
  juego del Ángel, El 104
  sombra del viento, La 103

Saltero, Víctor 106–9
  amante de la belleza, El 107–9
  Sucedió en el Ave 107–8
  Sucedió en la Moncloa 107
Salvador, Tomás 8
  charco, El 7
Santiago de Compostela 46, 61–2
Savater, Fernando 14, 45
  Caronte aguarda 14, 45

Sayers, Dorothy L. 10
Scotland Yard 7
Sedmay Ediciones 77
Serra, Antoni 11, 57
Silva, Lorenzo 18–20, 24 n., 81, 102–3
  Carta blanca 102
  Lejano pais de los estanques 24 n.
  Nadie vale más que otro 24 n.
  Niebla y la doncella 24 n.
  Reina sin espejo, La 24 n.
Simenon, Georges 10, 32
Simó, Isabel-Clara 87–8
  ombra fosca com un núvol de tempesta, Una 87–8
Sjoholm, Barbara (prev. Wilson) 83–4
social novel (Spanish) 9
space
  cultural 31, 33, 52
Spanish Civil War 2, 4, 6–7, 9, 19, 29, 36, 53, 76, 86–7, 100–4
Spanish Inquisition 7
Sûreté 7

Tasis, Rafael 9, 11, 20, 56
Tejero Molina, Antonio 19
terrorism 24, 51
Thorne, Kirsten 9
Torre, de la Josefina (pseud. Laurade Comingas) 76
  enigma de los ojos grises, El 76
Torrent, Ferran 11, 57
  isla del holandé, La 23 n.
  mirada del Tafur, La 23 n.
  No emprenyeu el comissari 22 n.
  Penja el guants Butxana 22 n.
  Semental, estimat Butxana 22 n.
  Societat limitada 23 n.
  negre amb un saxo, Un 22 n.
  vida en el abismo, La 22 n.
Torres, David 98–100, 110
  gran silencio, El 98–9, 110–12
  Niños de tiza 99
Transición 36–7, 40
Trapiello, Andrés 45, 99–101, 103
  amigos del crimen perfecto, Los 45, 100

Umbral, Francisco 12

Vázquez de Parga, Salvador 10, 75
Vázquez Montalbán, Mañuel 3, 13, 28–50, 51, 93, 95, 97–8, 136
   mares del Sur, Los 34–5, 39–42, 45–7
   Tatuaje 13, 23 n., 29, 44, 94
   Yo maté a Kennedy 23 n,, 28, 94

Viegas, Francisco José 126, 131–41
   Duas Águas do Mar 133–41

Young, Alison 52

Zarraluki, Pedro 101, 103
   encargo difícil, Un 101–2
Zorrilla, José 1
   'testigo de bronce, Un' 1